Information Agglomeration of Japanese Auto Parts Suppliers

Yosuke Takeda · Ichihiro Uchida

Information Agglomeration of Japanese Auto Parts Suppliers

Springer

Yosuke Takeda
Department of Economics
Aichi University
Nagoya, Aichi, Japan

Sophia University
Tokyo, Japan

Ichihiro Uchida
Department of Economics
Aichi University
Nagoya, Aichi, Japan

ISBN 978-981-19-3299-1 ISBN 978-981-19-3300-4 (eBook)
https://doi.org/10.1007/978-981-19-3300-4

This Springer imprint is published by the registered company Springer Nature Singapore Pte Ltd.
The registered company address is: 152 Beach Road, #21-01/04 Gateway East, Singapore 189721, Singapore

Preface

Professor Cesar Hidalgo's 2015 book, *Why Information Grows*, "describe(s) the economy as the system by which people accumulate knowledge and knowhow to create packages of physical order, or products, that augment our capacity to accumulate more knowledge and knowhow and, in turn, accumulate more information" (p. 8). According to his views on the growth of information, each product embodies the "crystallized imagination" of people as a fundamental embodiment of knowledge, so that quantization of knowhow or knowledge is restricted by "personbytes" and "firmbytes" of information capacities. In order to overcome these limits, there should be a network structure for information sharing, both spatially and organizationally.

This eBook reconsiders the idea proposed by Hidalgo (2015) as a new concept of "information agglomeration"; our neologism represented by industrial agglomeration within cities or innovation clusters embodying external increasing returns to scale. According to the conventional economics of transaction costs pioneered by Ronald Coase and Oliver Williamson, however, dispersed organizational networks for information sharing would be expensive to form and sustain.

Our book raises an important research question: what lowers transaction costs associated with organizational links for information agglomeration? To find an answer to this fundamental question, an industrial organization (IO) foundation for the concept of information agglomeration is constructed based on the transaction-cost approach to organizational networks, instead of the principal-agent approach to private information revelation. The transaction-cost models are also empirically tested by some structural estimations using establishment-based microdata of Japanese auto parts suppliers, which exemplify a general-purpose technology along with automobile electronics.

Our empirical analyses suggest that technology cooperation among suppliers improves their productivity through knowledge/information sharing; for example, auto parts suppliers' initiative to acquire relation-specific skills by joining technological cooperation associations. Moreover, a nation-wide competition policy, even in countries with a comparatively lower degree of law and order, is effective under legal enforcement that publicly regulates coalitions for incumbents and promotes entrants' incentive to innovate.

The empirical evidence on the IO models of information agglomeration from Japanese auto parts suppliers indicates the need for institutional arrangements for information agglomeration to create a global value chain. These may include a role of technological cooperation associations in sharing relation-specific skills, preferably organized on the initiative of suppliers. The other arrangement for region- or nation-wide competition policy is a legal enforcement scheme that publicly regulates coalitions for incumbents and mitigates entrants' incentive to innovate. Both factors would be relevant to policymakers seeking to enhance firms' technological innovation capabilities to raise productivity.

Nagoya, Aichi, Japan

Yosuke Takeda
Ichihiro Uchida

Acknowledgements

This book consists of five chapters, including an ushering prefatory one; the four main chapters are based on our research work for a RIETI Discussion Paper Series independently written during 2009 and 2015. We want to thank the Research Institute of Economy, Trade and Industry (RIETI) for providing us with a platform to hold unfettered discussions about our research.

We also owe it to Prof. Cesar Hidalgo's inputs on a core concept of this publication. Author Takeda met him at the MIT Media Lab on July 17, 2017, and explained how Japanese auto parts suppliers had drawn our interest, and how Prof. Cesar's book had been an inspiration for this work. While compiling our *tetrabiblos* papers into a volume in 2019, we had a clear image of the concept and title of this eBook. We wish Prof. Cesar all the best for his new mission of learning collective intelligence at Toulouse, France.

The original papers of the volume have been presented at numerous conferences, including the 9th Comparative Analysis Enterprise Data (CAED) Conference 2009 in Tokyo, Japan; the Far Eastern and South Asia Meeting of the Econometric Society in Tokyo, Japan; and the 10th CAED and COST Conference 2010 in London, UK, for Chap. 2; the 62nd Annual Meeting of AFSE at Aix-en-Provence, France and Annual Meeting, AEA 2020, San Diego, US, for Chap. 3; the 11th CAED and COST Conference 2012 at Nuremberg, Germany, for Chap. 4; and the 64th Annual Meeting of AFSE at Rennes, France and the 7th European Conference on Corporate R&D and Innovation (CONCORDi 2019) in Seville, Spain, for Chap. 5. We are grateful to all the participants for their encouraging comments on each paper. We also want to acknowledge the research assistance and financial aids extended to us for participating in these events. We owe the completion of Chap. 4 entirely to the collaboration with Prof. Shirai Daichi of Tohoku Gakuin University; his computation skills were indispensable for the publication of this book.

Finally, we owe our intellectual stimulus to late Emeritus Professor Takeshi Ozeki of Sophia University, who always encouraged Takeda not to confine his interests only to economics but also physics, especially the network theory. I am also grateful to late Prof. Masayuki Otaki, University of Tokyo who has spurred me to keep up as a good economist since my graduation at University of Tokyo.

Contents

About the Authors

Yosuke Takeda Master of Economics (University of Tokyo), is Professor at the Faculty of Economics, Aichi University, Japan and Emeritus Professor of Sophia University, Japan. Prior to his current position, he was a Visiting Associate Professor at the Department of Economics, Rutgers University (1997); a Visiting Research Fellow at the Economic Growth Center, Yale University (1998, 2007); an Associate Professor at the Faculty of Economics, Sophia University (1994–2005); and a Professor at the Faculty of Economics, Sophia University (2006–2024).

His research interests cover macroeconomics including monetary policy and fiscal policy, empirical industrial organization of Japanese auto parts suppliers and supply chain networks, an evolutionary approach to intra-family risk-sharing, and a social learning model of state formation and cultural evolution. His research has been published in various academic journals including Macroeconomic Dynamics and the Japanese Economic Review. He has also published and contributed to books on heterogeneous expectations in the Japanese economy, effects of unconventional monetary policy, and other topics. He received the Economist Award in 2013 (Mainichi Shimbun), which was shared with Mr. Yasuhide Yajima. Research outputs are available at the following website: https://ideas.repec.org/f/pta207.html.

Ichihiro Uchida Ph.D. (Ritsumeikan University), is Professor at the Faculty of Economics, Aichi University, Japan. Prior to his current position, he was a Visiting Research Fellow at the Department of Economics, Okinawa International University (2016–2017); an Associate Professor at the Faculty of Economics, Aichi University (2002–2012).

His research interests cover applied econometrics analyses on regional industrial structure and regional finance; networks of Japanese auto parts suppliers; and family business succession in Okinawa, Japan. His research has been published in various academic journals including regional science and regional finance. Research outputs are available at the following website: http://ideas.repec.org/e/puc8.html.

Chapter 1
The Economics of Information Agglomeration

Contents

Abstract This chapter reviews some strands of economics literature concerning our research question, "what lowers transaction costs associated with organizational networks?" We give a brief summary of the following chapters.

Keywords Auto-parts supplier(s) · Information agglomeration · Hidalgo · cesar · Transaction cost(s) · Flexible specialization · Organizational network

1.1 Introduction

1.1.1 Information Agglomeration

Information as an invisible physical matter grows towards *physical order* against uncertainties. An ability to create physical order takes some form of idea or knowledge. The physics view on information seems to be different from the standard economics' one, as represented by the so-called "market for lemons" (Akerlof, 1970), which shows how informational asymmetries between buyers and sellers of products can make the market missing, or the use of knowledge in society (Hayek, 1945), where market mechanisms can play the role of an aggregator of knowledge into market prices. In economics, as complements to market prices, informational signals

Y. Takeda and I. Uchida, *Information Agglomeration of Japanese Auto Parts Suppliers*,
https://doi.org/10.1007/978-981-19-3300-4_1

for quality of traded goods and services transform a prior distribution of the signals into a posterior distribution conditional on the observation.

In contrast to the qualitative definition of information in economics, physics especially in information theory, defines information as a physical order quantitatively measured with entropy in a unit of bit. As Arrow (1974) pointed out, "The quantitative definition which appears in information theory is probably of only limited value for economic analysis, for reasons pointed out by Marschak: different bits of information, equal from the viewpoint of information theory, will usually have very different benefits or costs." (p. 38).

In the face of such an inconsistency between quantitative and qualitative definitions of information, Hidalgo (2015) fills in the gap so that he "describe(s) the economy as the system by which people accumulate knowledge and knowhow to create packages of physical order, or products, that augment our capacity to accumulate more knowledge and knowhow and, in turn, accumulate more information." (p. 8) According to Hidalgo's view on the growth of information, each product embodies the "crystallized imagination" of people as a fundamental embodiment of knowledge, so that quantization of knowhow or knowledge is restricted by "personbytes" and "firmbytes" of limits to information capacities. In order to overcome these limits, there should be a network structure for information sharing, both spatially and organizationally.

The chapter follows the idea of Hidalgo (2015) as our new concept of "*information agglomeration*" represented by industrial agglomeration within cities or innovation clusters as external increasing returns to scale, similar to the concept of "domain" as technological clustering in engineering (Arthur, 2009). Based on the conventional economics of transaction costs pioneered by Coase (1937) and Williamson (1985), however, dispersed organizational networks for information sharing would be costly for organizations to form and sustain. In the following chapters, a recurring research question is "what lowers transaction costs associated with organizational links for information agglomeration?" To find an answer, we build an industrial organization (IO) foundation for the concept and apply the transaction-cost models to Japanese auto-parts suppliers as an eligible case of empirical tests.

1.1.2 Japanese Auto-Parts Suppliers

The so-called Moore's Law states that the number of transistors per integrated circuit would double every 18 months. Similarly, the number of micro-controller units (MCUs) installed per vehicle has doubled every decade: for example, in so-called middle-class cars, it increased from 8 on an average in 1980 to 17 in 1990, 32 in 2000, and so on (YANO Research, 2009). "Automobile electronics" has dramatically changed the concept of automobiles, evolving from mechanical alignment to human anatomy, as depicted by Fig. 4.2 in Chap. 4. Consisting of a variety of auto-parts products,[1] automobile electronics makes full use of general purpose technologies (David, 1990; Jovanovic & Rousseau, 2005).

In 1970, automobile constructors responded to first-time emission controls imposed by the Muskie Act (the U.S. Clean Air Act), which aimed to reduce HC, CO, and NOx emissions by 90% each. The overly strict standards required Japanese constructors to make fuel efficiency and engine performance compatible with each other. Some Japanese automobile constructors developed "hybrid cars" with built-in devices for electronically controlled fuel injection: Toyota Motor Corporation launched the Prius in 1997, followed by Honda's Insight in 1999, and Nissan's Tino Hybrid in 2000.

Regarding an outcome of research and development held by constructors and suppliers of newly-required parts, we witness a change in a trend of market prices for both automobiles and auto parts (Fig. 4.1 in Chap. 4). The fluctuation in prices happened parallelly for both, with the relative prices holding relatively steady till 1995. During the second half of the nineties, however, motor vehicles encountered a spike in prices, which remained on a gradual upward trend thereafter. By contrast, prices of auto parts and accessories constantly decreased from the mid-eighties. The structural change in the relative prices of auto parts coincides with the prominent rise of automobile electronics.

We can address some microeconomic mechanisms in the development of general purpose technology, exemplified by the technological innovations by the Japanese auto-parts suppliers along with the rise of automobile electronics.

First, Piore and Sable (1984) pointed out that technological changes from mass-production mode, called Fordism, to a mode of limited manufacturing of diversified products are enabled by "flexible specialization." Flexible specialization can be described as the sharing of organizational capital within limited participants, and the coexistence of external competition and internal cooperation. Technological clusters are distributed across the US' Silicon Valley, where firms located close to one another learn innovations (Saxenian, 1996). Similarly, in 1997, Toyota Motor Corporation stepped in to help Aisin Seiki, a critical supplier of p-valves to Toyota, when a fire broke out at its Kariya plant in Japan and forced the supplier to stop production. Corporations affilated to Toyota, including member companies of its association for technology cooperation, came together to reproduce the parts manufactured by Aisin (Nishiguchi & Beaudet, 1998).

Second, Mokyr (2002) also hypothesizes functionally that technological progress maps from a Ω-type of propositional knowledge, invented by scientific inquiries and discoveries and retained in terms of personbytes or firmbytes, selectively to feasible sets of a λ-type of prescriptive knowledge accessed society-wide. Even

[1] We can list the products here: engine control; electro AT (automatic transmission)/CVT (continuously variable transmission); electronically-controlled suspension; ABS (antilock brake system); train control system; electronically-controlled 4WS (4-wheel steering); EPS (electronically-controlled power steering); airbags; corner- and back-SONAR (sound navigation and ranging); driver positional memory; ACC (fully-automatic climate control system); cruise control; RKE (remote keyless entry); navigation; digital meters; multiplex transmission; on-board ETC (electronic toll collection); in-car camera; NVD (night vision device); or tire-pressure monitoring system.

technology choices based on rational decisions are subject to political processes, which often signify technophobic resistance to new technological changes from labor unions, lobbyists, and bureaucratic organizations, including governments. The political economy aspect of technology also matters between incumbents and entrants in global value chains, where different countries have different legal enforcement schemes. Japanese auto-parts suppliers have entered countries that maintain a high degree of law and order and have legal origin historically transplanted, and frequently face antitrust lawsuits with enormous reparations. Among the top 10 host countries where Japanese auto-parts suppliers deployed between 2003 and 2005, the US, UK, Thailand, India, and Malaysia have common law traditions, while China, Taiwan, and the Republic of Korea are under the German legal origin of civil law, and Indonesia and Philippines come under the French civil law, as indicated in Table 5.1 in Chap. 5.

1.1.3 Our Maintained Hypotheses

According to the conventional economics of transaction costs, as suggested by Ronald Coase and Oliver Williamson, it is costly for corporate managers to form and sustain dispersed organizational networks where information agglomerates. Therefore, the questions that arise are: (1) what lowers the transaction costs associated with organizational links? (2) how are the lowered transaction costs related to flexible specialization as pointed out by Piore and Sable (1984) and the political economy aspects of technology choice suggested by Mokyr (2002)?

Based on the motivation, the following chapters of this volume aim to create an industrial organization (IO) foundation for information agglomeration, and empirically test the theoretical models in case of Japanese auto-parts suppliers. We use establishment-based microdata compiled by the Ministry of Economy, Trade and Industry, Japan: *Census of Manufactures*; *Basic Survey of Japanese Business Structure and Activities*; and *Basic Survey of Overseas Business Activities*. We also supplement these establishment-based microdata with the databases of industrial associations and public organizations: the Japan Auto Parts Industries Association's annual magazine *Japanese Auto Parts Industries*, the Japan Patent Office's *IP Gazettes*; the World Bank's *Worldwide Governance Indicators*; and the Transparency International's *Corruption Perceptions Index*.

We consider four hypotheses on what lowers transaction costs associated with organizational links for information agglomeration. We mention a brief summary of the results in the following chapters:

1. (Chapter 2) Technology cooperation among suppliers improves their productivity through knowledge/information sharing.
2. (Chapter 3) Auto-parts suppliers have probably designed initiatives to acquire relation-specific skills by joining technological cooperation associations.
3. (Chapter 4) Capital adjustment costs are higher in automobile electronics.

4. (Chapter 5) Competition policy even in countries with a lower degree of law and order is effective under a legal enforcement that publicly regulates coalitions for incumbents and mitigates entrants' incentive to innovate.

1.2 What Lowers the Transaction Costs Associated with Organizational Networks?

We describe the economics of information agglomeration, linking it to four hypotheses concerning the core question of what lowers the transaction costs associated with organizational networks.

1.2.1 Information Sharing in Technology Cooperation Associations

To explain why we raise the question "agglomeration or congestion?" in terms of productivity, among related literature in economic theory and management science, we briefly view the roles of "economic distance." Economic distance can be interpreted in several contexts: geographical, industrial, social/sociological, organizational, or legal. Literature covered from the viewpoint of economic distance, however, are confined to economic growth theory, spatial economics, industrial organization, productivity analysis, and management science.

Marshall (1920) emphasized the advantages of proximity for production in entrepreneurship with a provident yet immature view on industrial agglomeration through three channels: goods, people, and ideas.

> When an industry has thus chosen a locality for itself, it is likely to stay there long: so great are the advantages which people following the same skilled trade get from near neighborhood to one another. The mysteries of the trade become no mysteries; but are as it were in the air, and children learn many of them unconsciously. Good work is rightly appreciated, inventions and improvements in machinery, in processes and the general organization of the business have their merits promptly discussed: if one man starts a new *idea*, it is taken up by others and combined with suggestions of their own; and thus it becomes the source of further new *ideas*. And presently subsidiary trades grow up in the neighborhood, supplying it with implements and materials, organizing its traffic, and in many ways conducing to the economy of its material. (IV, X, 7, Marshall, 1920)

Among "externalities" through the three channels, as Scitovsky (1954) pointed out, there is a distinction between technological externalities and pecuniary ones. While the former deal with non-market interactions directly affected by production function of a firm, the latter refer to interactions through market mechanisms. For the sake of this chapter, our interest is in "technological externalities" in production function caused by proximity to "source of further new ideas."

The Marshallian externalities have often been addressed in the economic growth theory (for instance, Romer, 1986). Monopoly rights to "lean" production technology associated with superior world knowledge become barriers to international transferability of technology to proximate countries in technological closeness, delaying economic development (Parente & Prescott, 1994; Schmitz, 1989). In the cross-sectional empirical studies following Barro and Sala-i-Martin (1997), using some spatial econometric methods, spatial externalities of technological interdependence are analyzed in the convergence equation (Ertur & Koch, 2007), or the costs of transporting physical capital between countries are considered to re-evaluate the Barro-regression results (Conley & Ligon, 2002).

More directly in regional and spatial economics, including economic agglomeration within congested "cities" (Fujita & Thisse, 1996) or industrial agglomeration from increasing returns (Krugman, 1991), a variety of social interactions are analyzed. These include a model of social distance, where correlated with social distance between agents, social decisions such as educational attainment or child-bearing may reproduce social "class" stability (Akerlof, 1997). Some indices for plants' geographic concentration and "coagglomeration" are constructed based upon a model of location choice, in the case of US manufacturing industries (Ellison & Glaeser, 1997) and UK data (Duranton & Overman, 2005). Input–output relations also provide an economic distance measure that is used to characterize interactions between sectors (Conley & Dupor, 2003).

In industrial organization, empirical studies on production (Ackerberg et al. 2007) address such market outcomes as industry dynamics of firms' entry and exit (Olley & Pakes, 1996); industry dynamics from product switching (Bernard et al. 2006); R&D spillover through patents (Griffith et al., 2006; Bloom et al., 2007); or spillover effects of opening"million dollar plants" on incumbent plants (Greenstone et al. 2008). These analyses suggest that the degree of proximity in industries, products, or inputs is a key factor in industry dynamics or technological spillover. In a series of papers by van Biesebroeck (2002, 2003) on productivity in automobile assembly plants in north America, technology choice or the switch between heterogeneous mass or lean (flexible) production accounts for differences between US and Japanese automobile producers in complementarities of productivity (Milgrom & Roberts, 1990; van Biesebroeck, 2007).

In management science literature, complementarities in production are mathematically represented in supermodular function (Topkis, 1995). As evidence of the complementarities, firms located near one another at Silicon Valley learn innovations (Saxenian, 1996). Similarly, in addition to the fire in the Aisin Seiki in 1997 and the quick recovery above mentioned, there was another accident visiting Riken Corporation, located at Niigata Prefecture in Japan that the Mid Niigata Prefecture Earthquake directly hit in 2007. Riken Co. then shared near a half the market of an automobile engine part, piston ring. Not only Toyota but also all the other Japanese motor corporations had to stop their productions, but the break period was up to one week. The episodes remind management researchers of sociological "small worlds" framed by Watts (1999), where horizontal bypass between suppliers is usually effective in hierarchical cluster structures (Aoki, 1986; Rajan & Zingales, 2001).

In practice, the most prominent activity between proximate firms may be research collaboration. The collaboration network has typical forms of either "joint ventures and research corporations," or "joint R&D and technology exchange" (Hagedoorn, 2002). The first form of collaboration is found in a new firm, and is based on equity investment jointly contributed by the firms involved. For instance, Toyota Motor Corporation and Panasonic Corporation established a firm, Panasonic EV Energy Co. Ltd., on December 1996 at Kosai, Shizuoka Prefecture, Japan. It is within 18 km of Toyota's major assembly plant at Tahara. The new firm develops, manufactures, and sells Nickel metal hydride and lithium-ion rechargeable batteries for hybrid electric vehicles (HEVs) and pure electric vehicles (PEVs), the profits of which are distributed in proportion to the investments (Toyota 60% and Panasonic 40%). The second form of research collaboration, R&D partnerships, however, is relatively more dominant compared with joint ventures, especially in industries such as pharmaceuticals or information technology.[2]

Among comprehensive literature, the closest approaches to Chap. 2 are the ones estimating some form of productivity functions. Griffith et al. (2006) assume that productivity depends on the number of patent citations. van Biesebroeck (2002, 2003) emphasizes the differences in productivity between "lean" and "mass" production systems. Henderson (2003) also identifies local information spillover in plant-level production functions of US machinery and high-tech industries.

1.2.2 Suppliers' Initiative for Relation-Specific Skills

The property right approach to Coasian firm boundaries, pioneered by Hart and Moore (1990), has been developed in many applied fields such as industrial organization, banking theory, or macroeconomics, including Kiyotaki and Moore (1997). The property right approach to a firm's investment hold-up relies upon the incomplete contract theory, where since contracts cannot fully state possible contingency occurring between the agents concerned, non-contractible investments, even though efficient ex ante, generate ex-post quasi-rent among them. The inefficient quasi-rent leads to the hold-up problem in a bargain between them (Hart, 1995). The approach has gained popularity in theoretical developments and its applications to some fields (Segal & Whinston, 2013, for a comprehensive survey).

Despite the numerous studies on theoretical development, empirical analyses on the approach itself have been surprisingly rare (a recent survey is Lafontaine and Slade (2013)). There seem to be possible reasons for the lean heap. One is the difficulty in distinguishing between transaction cost economics (TCE) and the property rights theory (PRT). Another, though lesser, difficulty is in measuring "marginal" return to "non-contractible" investment, which is required for testing PRT.

---

[2] The evidence is from Hagedoorn (2002), which presents some international evidence using the MERIT-CATI database, an extensive survey on inter-firm alliances starting in 1960.

1.2.3 Auto-Electronics and Capital Adjustment Costs

In this section, we briefly describe some literature related to Chap. 4, especially business cycle theories in which technology changes play a major role. A few business cycle studies emphasize the effects of capital adjustment cost on reduced volatilities of macroeconomic variables. Although our chapter does not address the general equilibrium aspects of capital adjustment costs, our motivation is similar to that of the papers mentioned below. Rather, taking micro evidence of the effects of automobile electronics on auto-parts suppliers, this chapter quantitatively makes clear what type of capital adjustment cost matters in the face of technological changes such as automobile electronics, a fundamental issue largely ignored by extant literature.

Penrose (1959) considers the shortage of managerial resources as limits to firms' growth, due to thc "span of control" representing the number of subordinates a supervisor has in a hierarchical organization. Uzawa (1969) adopts Penrose's idea and incorporates into the neoclassical growth model, an adjustment cost function $\varphi(I, K) = \varphi\left(\frac{I}{K}\right)K$, where $\varphi\left(\frac{I}{K}\right) > 0$, $\varphi'\left(\frac{I}{K}\right) > 0$, and$\varphi''\left(\frac{I}{K}\right) > 0$.

The convex adjustment cost function, first-order homogeneous in respect to I and K pins down an optimal investment level I^* in the long run.

On assumptions of Uzawa's adjustment cost function as well as perfect competitions in product markets, Hayashi (1982) shows in theory an equivalence between the average Tobin's Q and marginal q. Hayashi (1982) also proposes a quadratic form of the convex adjustment cost function $\varphi(I, K) = \varepsilon\left(\frac{I}{K} - \upsilon\right)^2 K$. Unlike the Uzawa/Hayashi adjustment cost function depending on investment rate $\frac{I}{K}$, Christiano et al. (2005) make an alternative function depending on the growth rate of investment $\frac{I}{I_{-1}}$, $\varphi(I, I_{-1}) = \varepsilon\left(\frac{I}{I_{-1}} - 1\right)^2 I_{-1}$, which can generate volatile fluctuations in the US capital investments to be calibrated with their New Keynesian dynamic stochastic general equilibrium model.[3]

With regard to economic history, David (1990) addresses "productivity paradox" of such general purpose technology (GPT) as the invention of the electric dynamo at the turn of the nineteenth century, or the modern computer. GPTs "occupy key positions in a web of strongly complementary technical relationships that give rise to 'network externality effects' of various kinds, and therefore make issues of compatibility standardization important for business strategy and public policy (p. 356)." GPTs also possess some characteristics: the emergence of an extended trajectory of incremental technical improvement; a gradual and protracted process of diffusion into widespread use; and the confluence with other streams of technological innovation (Bresnahan & Trajtenberg, 1995).[4]

---

[3] Eberly et al. (2006) estimate the alternative adjustment cost function of either Hayashi (1982) or Christiano, Eichenbaum and Evans (2005) using the US company data of *Compustat*, which indicates a higher likelihood of the Hayashi type over the Christiano, Eichenbaum and Evans one.

[4] In an introductory chapter (Lipsey, Bekar and Carlaw, 1998) to *General Purpose Technologies and Economic Growth*, edited by Elhanan Helpman, GPT is defined as "a technology that initially has much scope for improvement and eventually comes to be widely used, to have many uses, and

Therefore, the properties of improvement, pervasiveness, and innovation spawning would require firms to learn by doing GPT and also improve GPT's increments. Like Arrow's (1962) seminal paper on learning by doing, Jovanovic and Rousseau (2005) incorporate into the final/capital goods two-sector model a learning process, $\mathrm{p} = \left(\frac{K}{B}\right)^{-\beta}$, meaning that as per Moore's Law, competitive supply of capital K under constant returns to scale leads to the price of capital p, which always equals the average cost of production depending on a constant B. An increase in the parameter β, indicating higher learning speed, would raise long-term growth, but in the transition, decrease the speed of convergence since a reduction of new capital price causes free riding and thus delayed diffusion lags.[5]

On the cause of the Great Moderation in the US economy, Justiniano and Primiceri (2008) quantify the relative contributions to reducing macroeconomic fluctuations. Among structural disturbances in a dynamic stochastic general equilibrium (DSGE) model, the key shock determining real GDP growth and volatility of inflation is "investment-specific technology shock." The investment-specific technology shock is a disturbance μ_t in capital accumulation $K_t = (1-\delta)K_{t-1} + \mu_t\left[1 - \varphi\left(\frac{I_t}{I_{t-1}}\right)\right]I_t$ with the adjustment cost function of Christiano et al. (2005). The investment-specific technology shock can be interpreted as a shock to the relative price of investment in terms of consumption goods, or a shock to the production technology of capital goods (Greenwood et al., 1997).

Hornstein and Krusell (1996) also show that the investment-specific technological change may be a cause of the productivity paradox, in a vintage capital model where new technologies with less learning or less experience are introduced at a fast rate. Since learning or experience does matter for productivity, the investment-specific technology shock can then reduce measured productivity growth.

1.2.4 Legal Enforcements for Competition Policy

Debates on competition and innovation date back to the great divide between Joseph Schumpeter and Kenneth Arrow. Schumpeter (1942) took a stand against competition, saying, "The firm of the type that is compatible with perfect competition is in many cases inferior in internal, especially technological, efficiency." (p. 106). He argued that destroying profits after innovation, competition reduces firms' incentives to innovate to get into the *ex-post* market structure. However, advocating competition for innovation, Arrow (1962) said, "The pre-invention monopoly power acts as a strong disincentive to further innovation." (p. 620). He emphasized the *ex-ante* market structure, where more competition destroys profits before innovation and gives firms a greater incentive to innovate to escape from that state.

to have many Hicksian and technological complementarities."(p. 43). However, none of the formal definitions based on theoretical models has been established yet.

[5] For a comprehensive survey on general purpose technology, see Jovanovic and Rousseau (2005).

There are two related literatures on the motivation we follow. One is research on the dynamic effects of antitrust on innovation. A seminal paper of Segal and Whinston (2007) presents a dynamic model of antitrust in a winner-takes-all competition for product innovation, where the antitrust policy could be more protective of entrants from predatory behavior of incumbents reducing the entry probability in innovative industries. A dynamic consideration that Segal and Whinston (2007) address is the front-loading effect of antitrust policy on increased initial profits of potential entrants and on reduced "incumbency advantage" (Gans, 2011), that is, discounted expected profits of a continuing incumbent thereafter. Let us assume a competition policy outlawing the incumbent's practices that can reduce the probability of an entrant innovating. The profitability of such innovation-deterrent practices depends on the reduction of entrants' innovation; it is seen that the competition policy raises the rate of entrants' innovation due to the front-loading effect.

The other strand of related literature is the law and economics of endogenous legal enforcement (Glaeser & Shleifer, 2003; Schwartzstein & Shleifer, 2013). One of the issues addressed by this theory is litigation versus regulation, that is legal uncertainty necessitates regulation, instead of litigation. The possible schemes for legal enforcement are either strict liability, negligence, or regulation (Shavell, 1980; Kolstad et al., 1990; Cooter, 1991). A choice of legal enforcement endogenously generates optimal levels of R&D activities or deters them.

1.3 Concluding Remarks

We reviewed some strands of economics literature concerning our research question, "what lowers transaction costs associated with organizational networks?" Our empirical results suggest that technology cooperation among suppliers improves their productivity through knowledge/information sharing via auto-parts suppliers' initiatives to acquire relation-specific skills by joining technological cooperation associations. Moreover, competition policy even in countries with a lower degree of law and order is effective under a legal enforcement that publicly regulates coalitions for incumbents and mitigates entrants' incentive to innovate.

References

Ackerberg, D., Benkard, C. L., Berry, S., & Pakes, A. (2007). Econometric tools for analyzing market outcomes. In J.J. Heckman & E.E. Leamer (Eds.), *Handbook of econometrics* (vol.6, part A, ch.63, pp. 4171–4276). Elsevier

Akerlof, G. A. (1970). The market for 'lemons': Quality uncertainty and the market mechanism. *Quarterly Journal of Economics, 84*(3), 488–500.

Akerlof, G. A. (1997). Social distance and social decisions. *Econometrica, 65*(5), 1005–1027.

Aoki, M. (1986). Horizontal vs. vertical information structure of the firm. *American Economic Review*, 76(5), 971–983.

Arthur, W. B. (2009). *The nature of technology: What it is and how it evoloves*. Allen Lane.
Arrow, K. (1962). Economic welfare and the allocation of resources to invention. In *The Universities-National Bureau Committee for Economic Research and the Committee on Economic Growth of the Social Science Research Councils* (Ed.), *The rate and direction of inventive activity: Economic and social factors* (pp. 609–626). Princeton University Press.
Arrow, K. (1974). *The limits of organization*. W. W. Norton & Company.
Barro, R. J., & Sala-i-Martin, X. (1997). Technological diffusion, convergence, and growth. *Journal of Economic Growth, 2*(1), 1–26.
Bernard, A. B., Redding, S. J., & Schott, P. K. (2006). *Multi-product firms and product switching*. NBER Working Papers 12293.
Bloom, N., Schankerman, M., & Van Reenen, J. (2007). *Identifying technology spillover and product market rivalry*. NBER Working Papers 13060.
Bresnahan, T. F., & Trajtenberg, M. (1995). General purpose technologies 'Engines of growth'? *Journal of Econometrics, 65*(1), 83–108.
Christiano, L., Eichenbaum, M., & Evans, C. (2005). Nominal rigidities and the dynamic effects of a shock to monetary policy. *Journal of Political Economy, 113*(1), 1–45.
Coase, R. H. (1937). The nature of the firm. *Economica, 4*(16), 386–405.
Cooter, R. D. (1991). Economic theories of legal liability. *Journal of Economic Perspectives, 5*(3), 11–30.
Conley, T. G., & Dupor, B. (2003). A spatial analysis of sectoral complementarity. *Journal of Political Economy, 111*(2), 311–352.
Conley, T. G., & Ligon, E. (2002). Economic distance and cross-country spillover. *Journal of Economic Growth, 7*(2), 157–187.
David, P. (1990). The dynamo and the computer: An historical perspective on the modern productivity paradox. *American Economic Review, 80*(2), 355–361.
Duranton, G., & Overman, H. G. (2005). Testing for localization using micro-geographic data. *Review of Economic Studies, 72*(4), 1077–1106.
Eberly, J., Rebelo, S., & Vincent, N. (2006). *Investment and value: A neoclassical benchmark*. NBER Working Paper #13866.
Ellison, G., & Glaeser, E. L. (1997). Geographic concentration in US manufacturing industries: A dartboard approach. *Journal of Political Economy, 105*(5), 889–927.
Ertur, C., & Koch, W. (2007). Growth, technological interdependence and spatial externalities: Theory and evidence. *Journal of Applied Econometrics, 22*(6), 1033–1062.
Fujita, M., & Thisse, J. F. (1996). Economics of agglomeration. *Journal of the Japanese and International Economies, 10*(4), 339–378.
Gans, J. S. (2011). When is static analysis a sufficient proxy for dynamic considerations? Reconsidering antitrust and innovation. In J. Lerner & S. Stern (Eds.), *Innovation policy and the economy* (Vol. 11, pp. 55–78). MIT Press.
Glaeser, E. L., & Shleifer, A. (2003). The rise of the regulatory state. *Journal of Economic Literature, 41*(2), 401–425.
Greenstone, M., Hornbeck, R., & Moretti, E. (2008). Identifying agglomeration spillovers: Evidence from million dollar plants. *SSRN Electronic Journal*. NBER Working Papers, 13833.
Greenwood, J., Hercowitz, Z., & Krusell, P. (1997). Long-run implications of investment-specific technological change. *American Economic Review, 87*(3), 342–362.
Griffith, R., Harrison, R., & Van Reenen, J. (2006). How special is the special relationship? Using the impact of US R&D spillovers on UK firms as a test of technology sourcing. *American Economic Review, 96*(5), 1859–1875.
Hagedoorn, J. (2002). Inter-firm R&D partnerships: an overview of major trends and patterns since 1960. *Research Policy, 31*(4), 477–492.
Hart, O. (1995). *Firms contracts and financial structure*. Oxford University Press.
Hart, O., & Moore, J. (1990). Property rights and the nature of the firm. *Journal of Political Economy, 98*(6), 1119–1158.

Hayashi, F. (1982). Tobin's marginal q and average q: A neoclassical interpretation. *Econometrica, 50*(1), 213–224.
Hayek, F. A. (1945). The use of knowledge in society. *American Economic Review, 35*(4), 519–530.
Henderson, J. V. (2003). Marshall's scale economies. *Journal of Urban Economics, 53*(1), 1–28.
Hidalgo, C. (2015). *Why information grows: The evolution of order, from atoms to economies*. Basic Books.
Hornstein, A., & Krusell, P. (1996). Can technology improvements cause productivity slowdowns? In B. Bernanke & J. J. Rotemberg (Eds.), *NBER macroeconomics annual 1996* (pp. 209–259). MIT Press.
Jovanovic, B. & Rousseau, P. (2005). General purpose technologies. In P. Aghion & S. Durlauf (Eds.), *Handbook of economic growth*, vol. 1b. Elsevier BV, 1181–1224.
Justiniano, A., & Primiceri, G. E. (2008). The time-varying volatility of macroeconomic fluctuations. *American Economic Review, 98*(3), 604–641.
Kiyotaki, N., & Moore, J. (1997). Credit cycles. *Journal of Political Economy, 105*(2), 211–248.
Kolstad, C. D., Ulen, T. S., & Johnson, G. V. (1990). Ex post liability for harm vs. ex ante safety regulation: Substitute or complements? *American Economic Review*, 80(4), 888–901.
Krugman, P. (1991). Increasing returns and economic geography. *Journal of Political Economy, 99*(3), 483–499.
Lafontaine, F. & Slade, M. E. (2013). Inter-firm contracts: Evidence. In R. Gibbons & J. Roberts (Eds.), *Handbook of organizational economics* (pp. 958–1013). Princeton & Oxford: Princeton University Press.
Marshall, A. (1920). *Principles of economics*. MacMillan.
Milgrom, P., & Roberts, J. (1990). The economics of modern manufacturing: Technology, strategy, and organization. *American Economic Review, 80*(3), 511–528.
Mokyr, J. (2002). *The gift of Athena: Historical origins of the knowledge economy*. Princeton University Press.
Nishiguchi, T., & Beaudet, A. (1998). The Toyota group and the Aisin fire. *Sloan Management Review, 40*(1), 49–59.
Olley, G. S., & Pakes, A. (1996). The dynamics of productivity in the telecommunications equipment industry. *Econometrica, 64*(6), 1263–1297.
Parente, S. L., & Prescott, E. C. (1994). Barriers to technology adoption and development. *Journal of Political Economy, 102*(2), 298–321.
Penrose, E. (1959). *The theory of the growth of the firm*. John Wiley.
Piore, M. J., & Sabel, C. F. (1984). *The second industrial divide: Possibilities for prosperity*. Basic Books.
Rajan, R. G., & Zingales, L. (2001). The firm as a dedicated hierarchy: A theory of the origins and growth of firms. *Quarterly Journal of Economics, 116*(3), 805–851.
Romer, P. M. (1986). Increasing returns and long-run growth. *Journal of Political Economy, 94*(5), 1002–1037.
Saxenian, A. (1996). *Regional advantage: Culture and competition in Silicon Valley and Route 128*. Harvard University Press.
Schmitz, J. A., Jr. (1989). Imitation, entrepreneurship, and long-run growth. *Journal of Political Economy, 97*(3), 721–739.
Schumpeter, J. (1942). *Capitalism, socialism and democracy*. Harper & Brothers.
Schwartzstein, J., & Shleifer, A. (2013). An activity-generating theory of regulation. *Journal of Law and Economics, 56*(1), 1–38.
Scitovsky, T. (1954). Two concepts of external economies. *Journal of Political Economy, 62*(2), 143–151.
Segal, I., Whinston, M. D. (2013). Property rights. In R. Gibbons & J. Roberts (Eds.), *Handbook of organizational economics* (pp. 100–158). Princeton & Oxford: Princeton University Press.
Segal, I. R., & Whinston, M. D. (2007). Antitrust in innovative industries. *American Economic Review, 97*(5), 1703–1730.
Shavell, S. (1980). Strict liability versus negligence. *Journal of Legal Studies, 9*(1), 1–25.

Tokuda, A., & Saeki, Y. (2007). The automobile electronics (2): A market analysis of in-vehicle electronically-controlled system (in Japanese). *Ritsumeikan Business Journal, 46*(3), 55–90.
Topkis, D. M. (1995). Comparative statics of the firm. *Journal of Economic Theory, 67*(2), 370–401.
Uzawa, H. (1969). Time preference and the penrose effect in a two-class model of economic growth. *Journal of Political Economy*, *77*(4, Part 2), 628–652.
van Biesebroeck, J. (2002). The effect of technology choice on automobile assembly plant productivity. *Economic and Social Review*, 33(1), 65–73.
van Biesebroeck, J. (2003). Productivity dynamics with technology choice: An application to automobile assembly. *Review of Economic Studies, 70*(1), 167–198.
van Biesebroeck, J. V. (2007). Complementarities in automobile production. *Journal of Applied Econometrics, 22*(7), 1315–1345.
Watts, D. J. (1999). *Small worlds: The dynamics of networks between order and randomness.* Princeton University Press.
Williamson, O. E. (1985). *The economic institutions of capitalism: Firms, markets, relational contracting*. Free Press.
YANO Research. (2009). *In-vehicle semiconductor market 2009 & 2010 (in Japanese).*

Chapter 2
Technology Information Sharing

Contents

Abstract This chapter is in the spirit of (Marshall, Principles of economics, MacMillan, 1920), who raised the question of how economic distance affects a firm's productivity, focusing on the role of idea sharing in relation to technological knowledge or information between firms. In order to quantify the degree of knowledge spillover or information sharing, we take the production function approach. Assuming core-periphery structure around automobile assemblies surrounded with auto-parts suppliers, we estimate plant-level production functions of Japanese auto-parts suppliers, where the productivity function depends upon the degree of information sharing measured by both geographical plant location and membership of

This chapter is based on Takeda and Uchida "Technological Externalities and Economic Distance: A case of the Japanese automobile suppliers," RIETI Discussion Paper Series 09-E-051. We are grateful to: Mika Sato, Maki Yamaguchi, and Manami Fujishiro for their devoted assistance in data construction; Iichiro Uesugi and Toshiyuki Matsuura for their helpful suggestions on data accessibility and handling; Masahisa Fujita, Kyoji Fukao, Shin-ichi Fukuda, Futoshi Narita, Takatoshi Tabuchi, and Toyoharu Takahashi for their encouraging comments; and to numerous participants in the 9th Comparative Analysis Enterprise Data (CAED) Conference, 2009, and the Far Eastern and South Asia Meeting of the Econometric Society; the Research Institute of Economy, Trade and Industry; Development Bank of Japan; Nagoya University; and Nanjing University. We also appreciate the financial support from grant-in-aid for scientific research (#19,530,254), Ministry of Education, Culture, Sports, Science and Technology.

Y. Takeda and I. Uchida, *Information Agglomeration of Japanese Auto Parts Suppliers*,
https://doi.org/10.1007/978-981-19-3300-4_2

technological cooperation associations. We consider econometric issues of cross-sectional dependence of productivity and a simultaneity problem between inputs, applying methods to the standard ordinary least squares and generalized method of moments estimators. Positive technological externalities are seen in general and for independent plants, which is robust to specifications of the production functions. Agglomeration effects are, however, rarely observed for relation-specific or cooperative plants. Some of them cost substantial negative externalities. Once a simultaneity problem is econometrically considered, instead of increasing returns, decreasing returns to scale emerge in case of total materials. Agglomeration, if any, could be brought about not by increasing returns to scale, but by productivity spillover among suppliers proximate to automobile assemblies.

Keywords Information sharing · Agglomeration · Technological externality · Productivity · Cross-sectional dependence · Simultaneity · Automobile supplier

2.1 Introduction

Spatial and growth economics look to the productivity of firms as a primary driving force of economic development. Consequently, productivity analysis investigates how to quantify the unobservable matter and capture the effects on economic development. However, while the measurements of productivity are well understood, relatively little is known about how economic distance productivity and firm growth, although the question raised by Marshall (1920) is still relevant.

The chapter considers a role of economic distance in lowering transaction costs associated with organizational links for information agglomeration, as introduced in Chap. 1 and Hidalgo (2015). Technology cooperation among suppliers improves their productivity through knowledge/information sharing. For instance, Toyota Motor Corporation is famous for its "just-in-time" production system, where the make-to-order system aims to reduce goods-in-process inventories of automobile parts provided by Japanese circumvoluting suppliers. The domestic production system supported mainly by suppliers based in the Mikawa area at the center of Aichi Prefecture, however, has changed in the form of a step-up in overseas production. Between 1999 and 2008, the total automobile production rose more than 1.7 times, while there was a gradual decline in the domestic production ratio of manufactured automobiles from 65.9 to 48.9%. Will the decentralization of Toyota's producer regions make the Japanese giant more competitive globally as well as in the domestic market? Will domestic R&D jointly involving local suppliers be replaced with arm's-length patent license granted across the borders? The answers to these questions could hinge upon the distributions of productivity shared by auto suppliers in the periphery of automobile assembly plants. If the productivity distributions agglomerate into a mass or group, the organizational decentralization would reduce competitiveness. However, if the distributions reveal congestion in the neighborhood of core assemblies, the replacement of R&D with granted patent license would enhance productivity.

In this chapter, we estimate the production functions of Japanese auto-parts plants, specifying the relation between productivity and some measured economic distance. The estimations consider some econometric issues. Our main results are as follows:

1. In 2003, the number of companies with membership of associations for technology cooperation was limited. Most of the auto-parts corporations were independent of memberships.
2. The location distribution of general or independent plants is positively skewed. However, relation-specific or cooperative plants show differences in locations between automobile assembly groups or association memberships for technology cooperation.
3. The general or independent plants could benefit from positive technological externalities. Agglomeration effects of relation-specific or cooperative plants are rarely noticed for Japanese automobile corporations and their technology cooperation associations. A few of them cost the auto-parts plants or member companies substantial negative externalities in productivity.
4. Qualitative results concerning agglomeration or congestion vary between the standard OLS or GMM estimators and an estimator with cross-sectional dependence (Conley, 1999). However, general, relationship group, or independent plants still achieve agglomeration effect on auto-parts plants. The agglomeration effect of general and independent locations is also robust to specifications of production function in material variables and in cross-sectional dependence of productivity.
5. Once a simultaneity problem associated with unobservable productivity is econometrically considered, decreasing returns to scale emerge instead of increasing returns. Material variables also lose significance in estimating production functions. The rejection of constant returns to scale leads to agglomeration, if any, brought about not by increasing returns to scale, but by productivity spillover among proximate suppliers around automobile assemblies.

The chapter is organized into the following sections. Section 2.2 presents a brief overview of the role of economic distance in economic theory and management science. Based on the definitions of economic distance detailed in the Appendix, we construct some distance variables from data on plants' location and memberships with associations for technology cooperation. In Sect. 2.3, the production functions augmented with the productivity function are estimated with OLS and GMM estimators. The specification of the productivity function nests some types of agglomeration and congestion effects. Section 2.4 considers a few econometric issues associated with either cross-sectional dependence of productivity or a simultaneity problem between inputs. Finally, we conclude in Sect. 2.5.

2.2 Economic Distance in Theory and Practice

Though the concept of economic distance can be interpreted within broader contexts, we briefly introduced the concept with literature on economic growth theory, spatial economics, industrial organization, productivity analysis, and management science in Sect. 1.2.1 of Chap. 1.

2.2.1 Data Construction

We construct some measures of *economic distance* d_i applied to each plant i. We assume a core-periphery structure around automobile constructors surrounded with auto-parts suppliers. In the structure, technological information can be shared both by locating plants with geographical closeness and joining technological cooperation associations organized by auto assemblies.

Our data source of geographical distance is the *Census of Manufactures*, conducted by the Ministry of Economy, Trade and Industry, Government of Japan. We use a cross-section of data for the fiscal year 2003, when the Japanese macro economy had recovered from a severe deflationary episode. We pick up two broad items for auto parts: automotive body and concomitant of an industrial sub-classification 3012; and automotive component and accessory of 3013. We choose the following 10 companies, listed in alphabetical order, as the automobile constructors: Daihatsu, Hino, Honda, Isuzu, Matsuda, Mitsubishi, Nissan, Subaru, Suzuki, and Toyota. As described in the Appendix, our data excludes automobile assemblies, a 4-digit industrial sub-classification 3011, but the real constructor or group names are stipulated to be confidential in utilizing the plant-level data. Note that a subscript j denoting automobile production companies does not correspond to the order above.

The other data source is *The Japanese Auto Parts Industries*, published by the Japan Auto Parts Industries Association. It contains membership of each auto-parts company belonging to the technological cooperation associations organized by eight constructors (Daihatsu; Hino; Isuzu; Matsuda; Nissan; Subaru; Suzuki; Toyota) and the business partners of Honda and Mitsubishi.

We integrate both data sources to construct four measures of economic distance with the following definitions:

Definition 1 General: Minimum distance of a plant i measured from any automobile construction plants affiliated with 10 major production companies.

$$d_i^g \text{ for a plant} i \tag{2.1}$$

Definition 2 Relationship: Minimum distance of a plant ***i*** from any plant of either automobile production company above $j = 1{,}2,\ 3{,}4,\ 5{,}6,\ 7{,}8,\ 9,\ \text{or} 10.$

$$d_{i,j}^r \text{for a plant } i \text{and a company} j \tag{2.2}$$

I where consequently $d_i^g = \min_j d_{i,j}^r$.

Definition 3 Cooperation: Measured with the following product term:

$$\mathrm{d}_{\mathrm{i,j}}^{\mathrm{c}} \equiv \mathrm{d}_{\mathrm{i,j}}^{\mathrm{r}} \times (1 - \mathrm{dum_j})\text{for a plant} i \text{and a company } j \tag{2.3}$$

where dum_j *is a dummy variable consisting of a value* 1 *in case of each company joining a technology cooperation association organized by an automobile production company above* $j = 1{,}2, 3{,}4, 5{,}6, 7{,}8, 9,$ or10, *or a value* 0 *otherwise.*

If two suppliers join the same association organized by a constructor, they can share the technological information, so that the minimum distance of the plants from the constructor's establishment should be zero.

Definition 4 Independence: A measure for non-affiliating companies or plants with any specific automobile production companies.

$$d_j^i \equiv d_i^g \times dum_{-j} \tag{2.4}$$

where a dummy variable dum_j denotes technologically independent plants without cooperative relationships with any production companies $j = 1, 2, 3, 4, 5, 6, 7, 8, 9, or 10$.

Concerning the economic distance measures summarized in Table 2.14, there are a few characteristics to mention. First, we plot plant locations of our sample on the virtual globe software, Google Earth; the longitude and latitude are coded with geographical information software ArcGIS. Figure 2.1 indicates location information on plants joining any technology cooperation association organized by either automobile assembly corporation, that is plants with zero value of $d_{i,j}^c$. Compared with Fig. 2.2 of independent companies' locations, we find that the number of member companies of the associations is very limited.

Second, some histograms indicate that distribution of the general or independence distance measure is positively skewed (Figs. 2.3 and 2.4). The relationship or cooperation distance measures show differences between automobile assembly corporations (as typical cases, Figs. 2.5, 2.6 and 2.7), or between the groups for technology cooperation (similarly, Figs. 2.6 and 2.8).

2.3 Production Functions Estimated

This chapter estimates the Cobb–Douglas type of production function, measuring gross revenue y_i with an i.i.d. componentη_i,

$$\ln y_i = \beta_0 + \beta_k \ln k_i + \beta_l \ln l_i + \beta_m \ln m_i + \omega_i + \eta_i \tag{2.5}$$

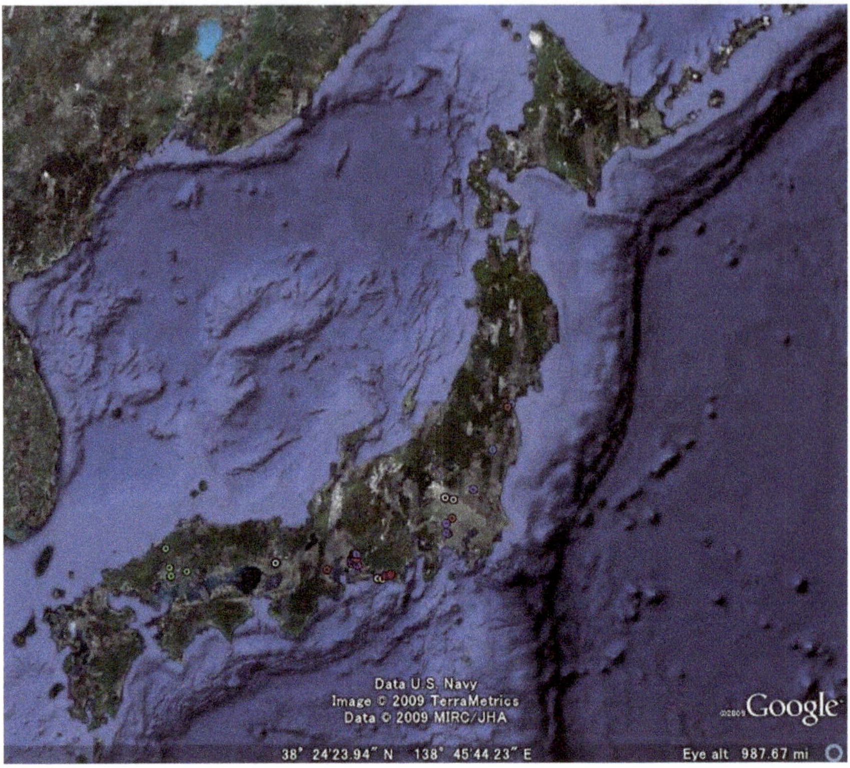

Fig. 2.1 Plant locations joining any technology cooperation association organized by either automobile assembly company $j = 1, \cdots, 10$

where capital stocks k_i, labour inputs l_i, and intermediate materials m_i are the production factors. Productivity of a plant i is then measured with the estimates $\widehat{\beta_0} + \widehat{\omega_i}$. Note that the Cobb–Douglas type of production function satisfies the supermodularity formulated by Topkis (1995).

We decompose the serially correlated component of productivity ω_i into two parts,

$$\omega_i = \omega_i^d + \omega_i^{-d} \tag{2.6}$$

where ω_i^d denotes distance-dependent productivity, and ω_i^{-d} means the residual productivity independent of economic distance. We assume that the distance-dependent productivity ω_i^d is exogenous, so that location choice of each plant or corporation is predetermined ahead of production decisions, including input choices. We recognize that plant location is another choice variable for corporations, as market entry and exit are endogenous decisions. However, as in the above citation from Marshall (1920), "When an industry has thus chosen a locality for itself, it is likely to stay there long: so great are the advantages which people following the same

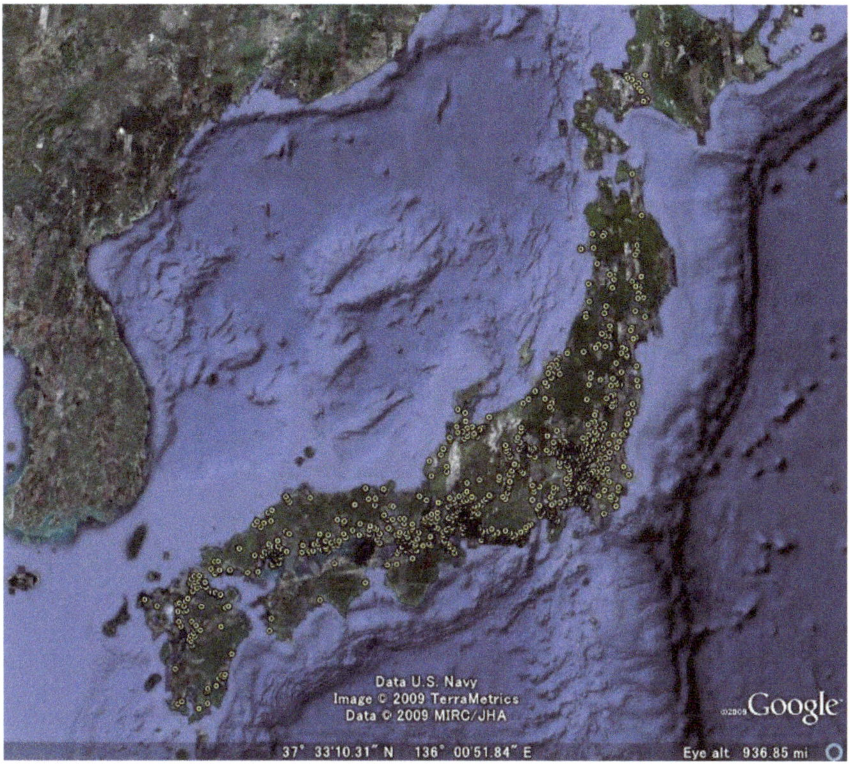

Fig. 2.2 Locations for plants independent of any technology cooperation association organized by either automobile assembly company $j = 1, \cdots, 10$

skilled trade get from near neighborhood to one another," the location choice is probably associated with sunk costs. The assumption is also appropriate for us since this chapter analyzes cross-sectional data.

2.3.1 Specification of Productivity Function

We approximate ω_i^d with a third-order polynomial in distance d_i.

$$\omega_i^d = \alpha_1 d_i + \alpha_2 (d_i)^2 + \alpha_3 (d_i)^3 \tag{2.7}$$

where a distance measure d_i is one among the four types of economic distance described above. Our simplified specification of the productivity function draws upon the Silicon Valley hypothesis of Saxenian (1996) that is, nearby firms learn innovations.

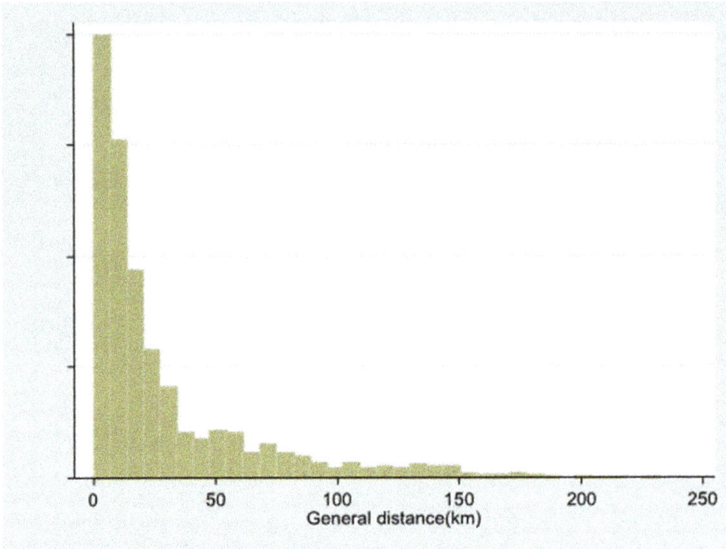

Fig. 2.3 Histogram of "general" distance

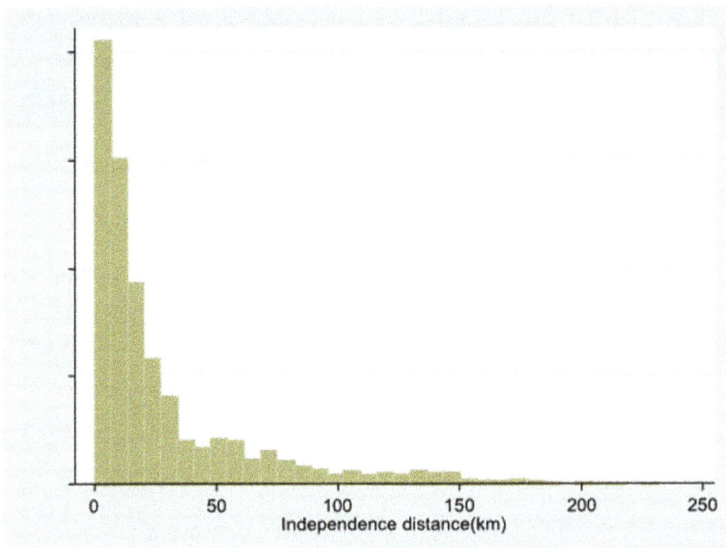

Fig. 2.4 Histogram of "independence" distance

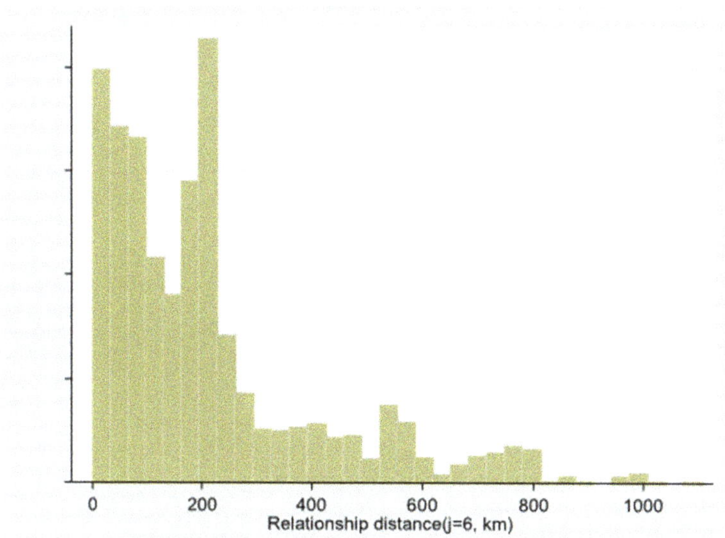

Fig. 2.5 Histogram of "relationship" distance (j = 6)

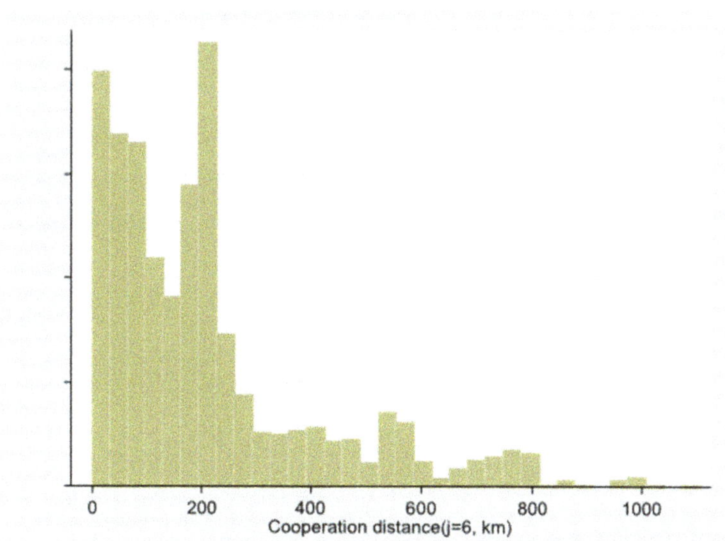

Fig. 2.6 Histogram of "cooperation" distance (j = 6)

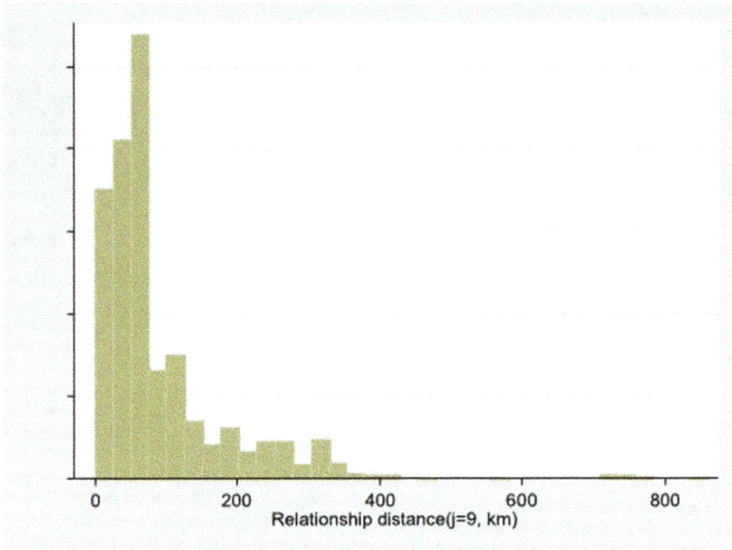

Fig. 2.7 Histogram of “relationship” distance (j = 9)

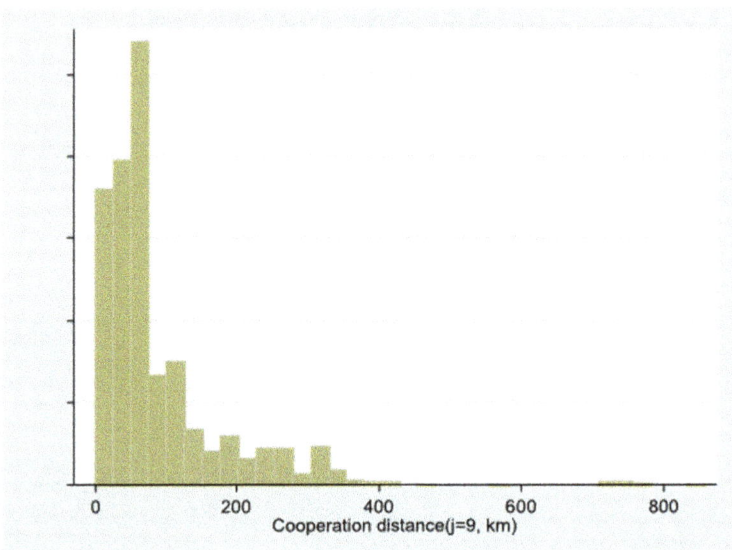

Fig. 2.8 Histogram of “cooperation” distance (j = 9)

Note that in the polynomial function, the distance measures and either input variables should be independent of each other. The constant predetermined locations cannot be state variables determining endogenous production inputs. In some cases, the distance measures are also the result of location choices by parent companies, which is out of scope for each plant.

Applying the specification of productivity function, we define the agglomeration and congestion effects. Agglomeration (congestion) has the same meaning as positive (negative) technological externalities defined by Scitovsky (1954). We evaluate the externalities in a neighborhood of core automobile assemblies, that is when$d_i + 0$. In our interpretation, the congestion effect, for instance, indicates a "lock-in-effect" preventing suppliers from getting access to more advanced technology provided by more remotely located constructors.

Definition 5 The agglomeration effect on productivity in the sphere of any core assemblies is measured with signs of the estimates in the following cases:

A-1.Linear agglomeration:

$$\left.\frac{d\omega_i^d}{d(d_i)}\right|_{\to +0} = \widehat{\alpha_1} < 0$$

A-2.Quadratic agglomeration:

$$\left.\frac{d\omega_i^d}{d(d_i)}\right|_{\to +0} = \widehat{\alpha_1} = 0 \;\Lambda\; \left.\frac{d^2\omega_i^d}{d(d_i)^2}\right|_{\to +0} = 2\widehat{\alpha_2} < 0$$

A-3.Cubic agglomeration:

$$\left.\frac{d\omega_i^d}{d(d_i)}\right|_{\to +0} = \widehat{\alpha_1} = 0 \;\Lambda\; \left.\frac{d^2\omega_i^d}{d(d_i)^2}\right|_{\to +0} = 2\widehat{\alpha_2} = 0 \;\Lambda\; \left.\frac{d^3\omega_i^d}{d(d_i)^3}\right|_{\to +0} = 6\widehat{\alpha_3} < 0.$$

Definition 6 The congestion effect is also measured in the following cases:*C-1. Linear Congestion*:

$$\left.\frac{d\omega_i^d}{d(d_i)}\right|_{\to +0} = \widehat{\alpha_1} < 0$$

C-2. Quadratic Congestion:

$$\left.\frac{d\omega_i^d}{d(d_i)}\right|_{\to +0} = \widehat{\alpha_1} = 0 \;\Lambda\; \left.\frac{d^2\omega_i^d}{d(d_i)^2}\right|_{\to +0} = 2\widehat{\alpha_2} < 0$$

C-3. Cubic Congestion:

$$\left.\frac{d\omega_i^d}{d(d_i)}\right|_{\to +0} = \widehat{\alpha_1} = 0 \;\Lambda\; \left.\frac{d^2\omega_i^d}{d(d_i)^2}\right|_{\to +0} = 2\widehat{\alpha_2} = 0 \;\Lambda\; \left.\frac{d^3\omega_i^d}{d(d_i)^3}\right|_{\to +0} = 6\widehat{\alpha_3} < 0.$$

2.3.2 OLS and GMM Estimates

We first show estimation results excluding any distance variable in the explanatory variables. Evidently in Table 2.1, the fit is well with R^2 at least 0.89. All the estimated coefficients on production inputs are significant, though the relative magnitude is different between two cases with total or raw materials as an explanatory variable. The null hypothesis of constant returns to scale (CRTS) $\beta_k + \beta_l + \beta_m = 1$ is strongly rejected in all the cases, which implies increasing returns to scale in the Japanese auto-parts plants.

We estimate the production functions augmented by the economic distance measures with OLS and GMM estimators. The GMM estimator instruments the first lagged variables of endogenous production inputs, labor, capital stocks, and materials. The instrument data is supplemented by the sample of year 2002. We alternate either variable of total materials, including raw materials, fuel, electricity and outsourcing costs, or raw materials. Heteroskedasticity robust standard errors are the ones proposed by Davidson and MacKinnon (2004).

We proceed to estimating each equation augmented by the productivity function of each economic distance variable one by one. The magnitude and significance of the coefficients on inputs remain almost the same as in the production function without distance. The increasing returns to scale are also accepted. Results on the coefficients in the productivity function are in Table 2.4 for OLS estimates and Table 2.5 for GMM. Qualitative results of OLS are very similar to those of GMM. We make some remarks about the GMM results.

Table 2.1 OLS and GMM estimations without distance: product dummy variables controlling for demand effects

Variable (name)		Coefficient (Robust standard error)			
		OLS		GMM	
Labour (lnobe2)	β_l	0.68*** (0.04)	0.87*** (0.02)	0.70*** (0.5)	0.88*** (0.02)
Capital (lkstock2)	β_k	0.01*** (0.006)	0.03*** (0.007)	0.01** (0.006)	0.03*** (0.007)
Materials	β_m				
Total materials (lmtotal2)		0.41*** (0.03)	-	0.41*** (0.03)	–
Raw materials (lzairyo2)		–	0.24*** (0.01)	–	0.25*** (0.01)
Const	β_0	–2.38*** (0.27)	–3.12*** (0.23)	–2.52*** (0.30)	–3.23*** (0.22)
Returns to scale		55.84(0)	97.63(0)	55.04(0)	114.69(0)
R^2		0.92	0.89	0.92	0.89
# of obs		2346			

Note F statistics and p-value in a parenthesis for constant returns-to-scale

The results imply that general and independence distances do matter with positive technological externalities of plant location. The agglomeration effects of relationship and cooperation distances on productivity are only noticeable for some of the Japanese automobile corporations and their technology cooperation associations. A few of them cost the auto-parts plants or the member companies substantial negative externalities in productivity.

In the case of total materials, few of the economic distance measures are significant except for general distance, relationship and cooperation $j = 6$, and independence distance. In the estimated productivity functions of the four distance variables, we find the agglomeration effect of a type *A-1* defined above. However, raw materials generate more coefficients in the productivity polynomial, which are significant with a significance level of 10%. There are not only seven equations of the *A-1* agglomeration, including general, relationship and cooperation$j = 6$, and independence distance, and one equation of the *A-2* agglomeration effect, but also six of the *C-1* congestion effect; for instance, on the automobile assembly corporation$j = 3$. The remaining estimated equations also suggest neither the agglomeration nor the congestion effect.

2.3.3 Controlling for Demand Effects

Since some of the Japanese auto-parts suppliers at least probably maintain pricing power in their auto-parts markets, productivity term in estimated production function might contain changes in market demand for auto-parts. In order to control for products' market conditions, we include in production function the products dummy variables, which are equal to 1 if each auto-parts supplier list each product; or 0 otherwise. We cover total 28 items with 7-digit classification, subordinate to the 2 broader items of 4-digit auto-parts, automotive body and concomitant 3012 and automotive component and accessory 3013.

In order to make robust controlling for the demand effects, as the demand shifter we take two other alternatives to the product dummy variables used above. Instead of the product dummy variables, which cannot proxy for the pricing power held by each plant, we use the product share variables, defined as the product shares of a plant's shipment value to total shipment values summed over the sample plants. The share variables also involve the same 28 product items as the product dummy variables. If the auto-parts supplier does not list the products, the variables are equal to 0. Compared with Table 2.1 in the case of the product dummy variables, Table 2.2 of the product share variables does not indicate any significant changes in estimated coefficients on the production factors.

Some dominant plants would price their products probably at a higher level than the industry organization deflators we use to calculate real output values. The pricing power leads to over-estimation of the real output values on the left-hand side of the production function. Consequently, coefficients on either the product dummy or share

Table 2.2 OLS and GMM estimations without distance: product share variables controlling for demand effect

Variable (name)		Coefficient (Robust standard error)			
		OLS		GMM	
Labour (lnobe2)	β_l	0.65*** (0.04)	0.81*** (0.02)	0.66*** (0.04)	0.82*** (0.02)
Capital (lkstock2)	β_k	0.02*** (0.006)	0.03*** (0.007)	0.01** (0.006)	0.03*** (0.007)
Materials	β_m				
Total materials (lmtotal2)		0.41*** (0.03)	–	0.41*** (0.03)	–
Raw materials (lzairyo2)		–	0.26*** (0.01)	–	0.26*** (0.01)
Const	β_0	–1.94*** (0.28)	–2.41*** (0.25)	–2.08*** (0.31)	–2.50*** (0.24)
Returns to scale		24.45(0)	31.36(0)	25.56(0)	39.45(0)
R^2		0.92	0.89	0.92	0.89
# of obs		2346			

Note F statistics and p-value in a parenthesis for constant returns-to-scale

variable in the production functions should be positive. In the estimates of production functions with demand shifters, regardless of both OLS or GMM and total or raw materials, the dummy variables for the following products are significant with positive signs: gasoline engines for motor vehicles; parts of driving, transmission and operating units; car air-conditioners; and finished seats. As for the share variables with significantly positive coefficients, there are many products: passenger car bodies; special-use car bodies; diesel engines for motor vehicles; parts, attachments and accessories of internal combustion engines for motor vehicles; parts of driving, transmission and operating units; parts of chassis and bodies; finished seats; miscellaneous parts of motor vehicles, including parts of motorcycles; and knocked-down (KD) sets (passenger cars, buses, and trucks). The significance of these product dummy or share variables seems to capture the demand effects.

The other alternative of the demand shifter is products inventory variables, defined as ratios of a plant's inventory to shipment values of manufactured products. If suppliers do not manufacture the products, then the variables are equal to 0. While the products shares directly measure levels of market demand, the inventory ratios would be chosen by plants to smooth productions in the face of large variance in the products demand. Excluding the products with all the values 0, we use 20 product items, the number less than the products dummy and share variables. While the coefficients are presumed to be positive on the products dummy or share variable, those on the inventory ratios would be a priori obscure since the inventory ratios do not proxy for pricing power of plants, but variance of the products demand. Similarly, Table 2.3 shows significance of coefficients on each production factor.

Table 2.3 OLS and GMM estimations without distance: product inventory variables controlling for demand effects

Variable (name)		Coefficients (Robust standard error)			
		OLS		GMM	
Labour (lnobe2)	β_l	0.68*** (0.04)	0.87*** (0.02)	0.70*** (0.04)	0.88*** (0.02)
Capital (lkstock2)	β_k	0.02*** (0.006)	0.03*** (0.007)	0.01** (0.006)	0.03*** (0.007)
Materials	β_m				
Total materials (lmtotal2)		0.42*** (0.03)	–	0.41*** (0.03)	–
Raw materials (lzairyo2)		–	0.24*** (0.01)	–	0.25*** (0.01)
Const	β_0	–2.41*** (0.28)	–3.14*** (0.23)	–2.54*** (0.31)	–3.23*** (0.22)
Returns to scale		55.04(0)	100.19(0)	52.62(0)	119.62(0)
R^2		0.92	0.89	0.92	0.89
# of obs		2346			

Note F statistics and p-value in a parenthesis for constant returns-to-scale

From the similarities in the estimates among choices of the demand shifter, we will only show estimation results of all the cases with the products dummy variables as the demand shifter.

2.4 Econometric Issues

Estimates of productivity have been made by numerous analyses on estimation of production functions, especially influenced by Griliches and Mairesse (1998), who pointed out econometric problems associated with estimation of production functions using micro data. There are broadly two problems: cross-sectional dependence (Conley, 1999; Conley & Ligon, 2002) and simultaneity (Bond & Soderbom, 2005; Levinsohn & Petrin, 2003; Olley & Pakes, 1996).[1] We take the two econometric issues in the estimation.

[1] The reflection problem is also related to the estimation of production functions (Manski, 1993), in case endogenous social or peer effects are considered in the production process. There are cases of endogenous social effects of technology or location choice. Another possible problem is group effects on individual response variables in cluster sample (Moulton, 1990; Wooldridge, 2003). The Marshallian externalities in aggregate physical capitals are an example of the cluster effects.

Table 2.4 OLS estimations with distance

Distance order	Materials							
	Total				Raw materials			
	1st α_1	2nd α_2	3rd α_3	CRTS	1st α_1	2nd α_2	3rd α_3	CRTS
General								
	–0.006*** (0.001)	0.00008*** (0.00002)	–3.01e-07*** (7.31e-08)	54.16 (0)	–0.007*** (0.002)	0.00009*** (0.00002)	–3.47e-07*** (8.63e-08)	90.14 (0)
Relationship								
j = 1	–0.0004 (0.0007)	9.10e-07 (4.99e-06)	–5.58e-10 (1.03e-08)	55.57 (0)	–0.001 (0.0008)	4.66e-06 (6.14e-06)	–5.34e-09 (1.26e-08)	92.07 (0)
2	–0.0003 (0.0005)	1.52e-06 (1.93e-06)	–1.87e-09 (2.15e-09)	55.63 (0)	0.0003 (0.0005)	–6.44e-07 (2.07e-06)	–1.98e-10 (2.23e-09)	95.30 (0)
3	0.0003 (0.0002)	–4.94e-07 (4.32e-07)	1.32e-10 (2.45e-10)	55.58 (0)	0.0006** (0.0003)	–9.58e-07** (4.87e-07)	2.82e-10 (2.69e-10)	93.82 (0)
4	0.0003 (0.0002)	–7.92e-07 (5.69e-07)	5.54e-10 (4.18e-10)	55.68 (0)	0.0005* (0.0003)	–1.31e-06* (7.14e-07)	8.87e-10* (5.20e-10)	95.30 (0)
5	0.0001 (0.0003)	–6.86e-07 (8.07e-07)	4.01e-10 (5.60e10)	55.92 (0)	0.0004 (0.0003)	–1.65e-06* (8.92e-07)	1.04e-09* (6.13e-10)	94.37 (0)
6	–0.0005* (0.0003)	7.59e-07 (7.67e-07)	–3.18e-10 (6.14e-10)	56.17 (0)	–0.001*** (0.0003)	1.93e-06** (8.34e-07)	–9.95e-10 (6.58e-10)	89.80 (0)
7	0.0002 (0.0002)	–7.26e-07 (5.83e-07)	5.46e-10 (4.26e-10)	55.87 (0)	0.0005* (0.0003)	–1.57e-06** (7.30e-07)	1.12e-09** (5.32e-10)	95.38 (0)
8	0.0001 (0.0002)	–5.55e-07 (5.61e-07)	4.35e-10 (4.18e-10)	55.82 (0)	0.0003 (0.0002)	–1.16e-06* (7.03e-07)	8.48e-10 (5.23e-10)	95.72 (0)
9	–0.0007 (0.0005)	1.72e-06 (2.26e-06)	–1.34e-09 (2.26e-09)	56.03 (0)	–0.001** (0.0006)	3.56e-06 (2.56e-06)	–2.75e-09 (2.53e-09)	97.29 (0)

(continued)

Table 2.4 (continued)

Distance order	Materials							
	Total				Raw materials			
	1st α_1	2nd α_2	3rd α_3	CRTS	1st α_1	2nd α_2	3rd α_3	CRTS
10	0.0002 (0.0003)	–1.34e-06 (8.85e-07)	9.87e-10 (7.31e-10)	56.11 (0)	0.0002 (0.0003)	–1.55e-06 (1.02e-06)	1.20e-09 (8.08e-10)	95.16 (0)
Cooperation								
j = 1	–0.001 (0.0007)	5.94e-06 (5.28e-06)	–9.27e-09 (1.07e-08)	56.51 (0)	–0.001* (0.0008)	5.91e-06 (6.12e-06)	–7.44e-09 (1.26e-08)	91.49 (0)
2	–0.0003 (0.0004)	1.37e-06 (1.91e-06)	–1.75e-09 (2.13e-09)	55.52 (0)	0.0004 (0.0005)	–8.51e-07 (2.04e-06)	–1.78e-11 (2.21e-09)	95.53 (0)
3	0.0003 (0.0002)	–4.96e-07 (4.28e-07)	1.32e-10 (2.44e-10)	55.65 (0)	0.0006** (0.0002)	–9.58e-07** (4.81e-07)	2.80e-10 (2.67e-10)	94.38 (0)
4	0.0003 (0.0002)	–8.30e-07 (5.66e-07)	5.78e-10 (4.16e-10)	55.67 (0)	0.0005* (0.0003)	–1.34e-06* (7.09e-07)	9.11e-10* (5.17e-10)	95.57 (0)
5	0.0001 (0.0003)	–6.19e-07 (8.00e-07)	3.60e-10 (5.56e-10)	55.90 (0)	0.0004 (0.0003)	–1.51e-06* (9.02e-07)	9.42e-10 (6.17e-10)	94.57 (0)
6	–0.0005* (0.0003)	7.58e-07 (7.67e-07)	–3.17e-10 (6.14e-10)	56.17 (0)	–0.001*** (0.0003)	1.93e-06** (8.34e-07)	–9.93e-10 (6.58e-10)	89.80 (0)
7	0.0002 (0.0002)	–7.79e-07 (5.81e-07)	5.81e-10 (4.25e-10)	55.83 (0)	0.0005** (0.0003)	–1.64e-06** (7.26e-07)	1.16e-09** (5.30e-10)	95.59 (0)
8	0.0001 (0.0002)	–5.63e-07 (5.61e-07)	4.43e-10 (4.19e-10)	55.84 (0)	0.0003 (0.0002)	–1.06e-06 (7.06e-07)	7.94e-10 (5.24e-10)	95.99 (0)

(continued)

Table 2.4 (continued)

Distance order	Materials							
	Total				Raw materials			
	1st α_1	2nd α_2	3rd α_3	CRTS	1st α_1	2nd α_2	3rd α_3	CRTS
9	–0.0007 (0.0005)	1.53e-06 (2.22e-06)	–1.17e-09 (2.23e-09)	55.93 (0)	–0.001** (0.0006)	3.28e-06 (2.52e-06)	–2.49e-09 (2.50e-09)	96.62 (0)
10	0.0002 (0.0002)	–1.32e-06 (8.81e-07)	9.66e-10 (7.28e-10)	56.04 (0)	0.0001 (0.0003)	–1.52e-06 (1.01e-06)	1.18e-09 (8.04e-10)	94.93 (0)
Independence								
	–0.006*** (0.001)	0.00008*** (0.00002)	–3.03e-07*** (7.27e-08)	53.98 (0)	–0.008*** (0.002)	0.00009*** (0.00002)	–3.49e-07*** (8.55e-08)	89.42 (0)

Note F statistics and p-value in a parenthesis for constant returns-to-scale (CRTS)
* refers to significance at 10%, ** at 5%, and *** at 1% level

Table 2.5 GMM estimations with distance

Distance order	Materials							
	Total				Raw materials			
	1st α_1	2nd α_2	3rd α_3	CRTS	1st α_1	2nd α_2	3rd α_3	CRTS
General								
	–0.006*** (0.001)	0.00008*** (0.00002)	–2.96e-07*** (7.19e-08)	54.52 (0)	–0.007*** (0.002)	0.00009*** (0.00002)	-3.36e-07*** (8.43e-08)	106.02 (0)
Relationship								
j = 1	–0.0004 (0.0007)	8.16e-07 (4.97e-06)	–3.67e-10 (1.03e-08)	55.31 (0)	–0.001 (0.0008)	4.20e-06 (6.09e-06)	-4.70e-09 (1.26e-08)	109.31 (0)
2	–0.0003 (0.0004)	1.51e-06 (1.91e-06)	–1.87e-09 (2.13e-09)	54.83 (0)	0.0003 (0.0005)	–6.06e-07 (2.06e-06)	-2.21e-10 (2.22e-09)	112.86 (0)
3	0.0003 (0.0002)	–4.92e-07 (4.30e-07)	1.32e-10 (2.44e-10)	55.23 (0)	0.0006** (0.0002)	–9.03e-07* (4.86e-07)	2.56e-10 (2.69e-10)	111.40 (0)
4	0.0003 (0.0002)	–7.58e-07 (5.65e-07)	5.29e-10 (4.14e-10)	55.04 (0)	0.0004* (0.0003)	–1.24e-06* (7.07e-07)	8.37e-10 (5.15e-10)	112.49 (0)
5	0.0001 (0.0003)	–6.80e-07 (8.02e-07)	3.99e-10 (5.56e-10)	55.38 (0)	0.0004 (0.0003)	–1.62e-06* (8.83e-07)	1.00e-09* (6.07e-10)	111.66 (0)
6	–0.0005* (0.0003)	7.50e-07 (7.61e-07)	–3.12e-10 (6.10e-10)	55.60 (0)	–0.001*** (0.0003)	1.90e-06** (8.25e-07)	-9.91e-10 (6.48e-10)	106.93 (0)
7	0.0002 (0.0002)	–7.08e-07 (5.80e-07)	5.32e-10 (4.23e-10)	55.14 (0)	0.0005* (0.0003)	–1.50e-06** (7.27e-07)	-1.06e-09** (5.29e-10)	112.78 (0)
8	0.0002 (0.0002)	–5.24e-07 (5.57e-07)	4.12e-10 (4.15e-10)	55.11 (0)	0.0003 (0.0002)	–1.10e-06 (6.96e-07)	8.01e-10 (5.17e-10	112.84 (0)
9	–0.0008 (0.0005)	1.86e-06 (2.25e-06)	–1.47e-09 (2.25e-09)	55.42 (0)	–0.001** (0.0006)	3.67e-06 (2.54e-06)	-2.87e-09 (2.51e-09)	114.36 (0)

(continued)

Table 2.5 (continued)

Distance order	Materials							
	Total				Raw materials			
	1st α_1	2nd α_2	3rd α_3	CRTS	1st α_1	2nd α_2	3rd α_3	CRTS
10	0.0002 (0.0002)	–1.36e-06 (8.80e-07)	1.00e-09 (7.27e-10)	55.78 (0)	0.0002 (0.0003)	–1.57e-06 (1.00e-06)	1.20e-09 (7.98e-10)	113.01 (0)
Cooperation								
j = 1	–0.001 (0.0007)	5.74e-06 (5.24e-06)	–8.89e-09 (1.06e-08)	55.98 (0)	–0.001* (0.0008)	5.61e-06 (6.10e-06)	–7.07e-09 (1.26e-08)	108.80 (0)
2	–0.0003 (0.0004)	1.36e-06 (1.89e-06)	–1.74e-09 (2.11e-09)	54.73 (0)	0.0003 (0.0005)	–8.16e-07 (2.03e-06)	–3.77e-11 (2.20e-09)	113.11 (0)
3	0.0003 (0.0002)	–4.98e-07 (4.27e-07)	1.34e-10 (2.43e-10)	55.27 (0)	0.0006** (0.0002)	–9.06e-07* (4.80e-07)	2.55e-10 (2.66e-10)	111.98 (0)
4	0.0003 (0.0002)	–7.99e-07 (5.62e-07)	5.56e-10 (4.13e-10)	54.99 (0)	0.0004* (0.0003)	–1.28e-06* (7.02e-07)	8.65e-10* (5.12e-10)	112.74 (0)
5	0.0001 (0.0003)	–6.21e-07 (7.94e-07)	3.63e-10 (5.52e-10)	55.45 (0)	0.0004 (0.0003)	–1.46e-06 (8.93e-07)	9.07e-10 (6.11e-10)	111.98 (0)
6	–0.0005* (0.0003)	7.49e-07 (7.61e-07)	–3.11e-10 (6.10e-10)	55.60 (0)	–0.001*** (0.0003)	1.89e-06** (8.25e-07)	–9.89e-10 (6.48e-10)	106.94 (0)
7	0.0002 (0.0002)	–7.63e-07 (5.78e-07)	5.68e-10 (4.23e-10)	55.07 (0)	0.0005* (0.0003)	–1.56e-06** (7.23e-07)	1.11e-09** (5.27e-10)	112.97 (0)
8	0.0001 (0.0002)	–5.34e-07 (5.57e-07)	4.22e-10 (4.15e-10)	55.11 (0)	0.0003 (0.0002)	–9.90e-07 (6.98e-07)	7.43e-10 (5.19e-10)	113.02 (0)

(continued)

Table 2.5 (continued)

Distance order	Materials							
	Total				Raw materials			
	1st α_1	2nd α_2	3rd α_3	CRTS	1st α_1	2nd α_2	3rd α_3	CRTS
9	–0.0007 (0.0005)	1.65e-06 (2.21e-06)	–1.28e-09 (2.21e-09)	55.41 (0)	–0.001** (0.0006)	3.38e-06 (2.50e-06)	–2.60e-09 (2.48e-09)	113.58 (0)
10	0.0002 (0.0002)	–1.34e-06 (8.76e-07)	9.86e-10 (7.24e-10)	55.74 (0)	0.0002 (0.0003)	–1.55e-06 (9.99e-07)	1.18e-09 (7.94e-10)	112.80 (0)
Independence								
	–0.006*** (0.001)	0.00008*** (0.00002)	–2.98e-07*** (7.15e-08)	54.37 (0)	–0.007*** (0.002)	0.00009*** (0.00002)	–3.37e-07*** (8.35e-08)	105.13 (0)

Note F statistics and p-value in a parenthesis for constant returns-to-scale (CRTS)
* refers to significance at 10%, ** at 5%, and *** at 1% level

2.4.1 Cross-Sectional Dependence

We are concerned about the possibilities of interdependence among unobservable productivity in the plants, and its possible econometric influence on the OLS estimates above. We draw upon a non-parametric covariance matrix estimator proposed by Conley (1999). Conley (1999) applies the time-series method of Newey and West (1987) or White and Domowitz (1984) to cross-sectional data with possible spatial dependence characterized by economic distance. The covariance matrix estimators based upon GMM estimator are shown to be consistent even when economic distances are measured with errors. The key component reflecting the cross-sectional dependence lies in a weight matrix associated with spatial autocovariances, where the weights are used to calculate weighted averages of the spatial autocovariance terms. Considering the role of economic distance in ideas or knowledge, we suppose the weights are zero for plants located farther apart than some cut off levels L_x and L_y at longitude and latitude, respectively. More concretely, instead of a truncated estimator of White and Domowitz (1984), we take the following weight function $W_{xy}(j, k)$ of a Bartlett window (Newey & West, 1987), where a square regular lattice spaces each plant in square at longitude j and latitude k for $|j| < L_x, |k| < L_y$,

$$W_{xy}(j, k) = \begin{cases} \left(1 - \frac{|j|}{L_x}\right)\left(1 - \frac{|k|}{L_y}\right) & \text{for a plant in square at longitude } j \text{ and latitude } k \\ 0 & \text{otherwise.} \end{cases} \tag{2.8}$$

In setting the cutoff levels L_x and L_y in the weight function, we consider geographical information on the territory of Japan. Prefecture Hokkaido is located at the northernmost extreme, with the eastern end at longitude $148^\circ 53'42''$ and northern one at latitude $45^\circ 33'28''$. At the southernmost tip of continental Japan (excluding small-island shaped Okinawa Prefecture), Prefecture Kagoshima has a western end at longitude $128^\circ 23'43''$ and southern one at latitude $27^\circ 01'07''$. Considering the differences of the rectangular national land in longitude and latitude as well as the histograms displayed in Figs. 2.3, 2.4, 2.5, 2.6, 2.7 and 2.8, the cutoff levels for either longitude or latitude are set in the Conley (1999) method, at sample means of each distance measure multiplied with $\cos\left(\arctan\left(\frac{45-27}{148-128}\right)\right) \approx 0.743294$ or $\sin\left(\arctan\left(\frac{45-27}{148-128}\right)\right) \approx 0.668965$, respectively.

The results are shown in Table 2.6 for total materials and Table 2.7 for raw materials for OLS estimations of an equation without the productivity function. The OLS estimates are the same values whether with or without cross-sectional dependence. The spatial standard errors are of almost the same order as the heteroskedasticity robust standard errors for most of the variables, with the significance of the coefficients remaining unchanged in both cases of material variables.

Incorporating the productivity function in the equation, we examine the changes in the significance of the coefficients in the productivity function to check out whether there is agglomeration or congestion. Results are presented in Table 2.8 for total

Table 2.6 Cross-sectional dependence (1–1): OLS estimates (total materials)

Variable (name)		OLS estimate	Robust S.E	Spatial S.E
Labour (lnobe2)	β_l	0.68	0.04***	0.04***
Capital (lkstock2)	β_k	0.01	0.006***	0.004***
Materials (lmtotal2)	β_m	0.41	0.03***	0.03***
Const	β_0	–2.38	0.27***	0.26***
# of obs		2346		

Note * refers to significance at 10%, ** at 5%, and *** at 1% level

Table 2.7 Cross-sectional dependence (1–2): OLS estimates (raw materials)

Variable (name)		OLS estimate	Robust S.E	Spatial S.E
Labour (lnobe2)	β_l	0.87	0.02***	0.03***
Capital (lkstock2)	β_k	0.03	0.007***	0.007***
Materials (lzairyo2)	β_m	0.24	0.01***	0.01***
Const	β_0	–3.12	0.23***	0.27***
# of obs		2346		

Note * refers to significance at 10%, ** at 5%, and *** at 1% level

materials case and Table 2.9 for raw materials. Qualitative results concerning agglomeration or congestion are very different from the OLS estimates disregarding cross-sectional dependence. At a significance level of 10% in each case of total or raw materials, there are 6–10 functions of productivity with *C-1* type of congestion, while general, relationship $j = 1$, and independence distances still achieve agglomeration effect on the auto-parts plants. The agglomeration effect of general and independent locations is thus robust to specifications of the production function in material variables or in cross-sectional dependence of productivity.

2.4.2 *Simultaneity*

The GMM estimates above considered endogeneity of the explanatory input variables in the production function. However, there are no concerns about the simultaneity problem between the input variables. In the literature on productivity estimates, it has been known since Marschak and Andrews (1944) that a simultaneity problem is serious for estimating production function. The simultaneity problem occurs when there is contemporaneous correlation between unobservable productivity and production inputs. The simultaneity problem makes it difficult for econometricians to gain unbiased and consistent estimates. If capital stocks and labor input are positively

Table 2.8 Cross-sectional dependence (2–1): Total materials

Distance	Order	OLS estimate	Robust S.E	Spatial S.E
General	1st α_1 2nd α_2 3rd α_3	–0.006 0.00008 –3.007e-07	0.001*** 0.00002*** 7.31e-08***	0.002*** 0.00002*** 8.785e-08***
Relationship j = 1	1st α_1 2nd α_2 3rd α_3	–0.0004 9.102e-07 –5.585e-10	0.0007 4.99e-06 1.03e-08	0.00005*** 3.629e-07** 7.281e-10
j = 2	1st α_1 2nd α_2 3rd α_3	–0.0003 1.515e-06 –1.872e-09	0.0005 1.93e-06 2.15e-09	0.00003*** 1.395e-07*** 1.735e-10***
j = 3	1st α_1 2nd α_2 3rd α_3	0.0003 –4.944e-07 1.317e-10	0.0002 4.32e-07 2.45e-10	0.00001*** 2.530e-08*** 1.600e-11***
j = 4	1st α_1 2nd α_2 3rd α_3	0.0003 –7.921e-07 5.537e-10	0.0002 5.69e-07 4.18e-10	0.00001*** 2.312e-08*** 1.512e-11***
j = 5	1st α_1 2nd α_2 3rd α_3	0.0001 –6.863e-07 4.009e-10	0.0003 8.07e-07 5.60e-10	0.00002*** 4.793e-08*** 3.966e-11***
j = 6	1st α_1 2nd α_2 3rd α_3	–0.0005 7.593e-07 –3.180e-10	0.0003* 7.67e-07 6.14e-10	0.00002*** 6.968e-08*** 6.605e-11***
j = 7	1st α_1 2nd α_2 3rd α_3	0.0002 –7.264e-07 5.464e-10	0.0002 5.83e-07 4.26e-10	0.00001*** 2.568e-08*** 1.549e-11***
j = 8	1st α_1 2nd α_2 3rd α_3	0.0001 –5.546e-07 4.347e-10	0.0002 5.61e-07 4.18e-10	0.00001*** 2.290e-08*** 1.514e-11***
j = 9	1st α_1 2nd α_2 3rd α_3	–0.0007 1.722e-06 –1.341e-09	0.0005 2.26e-06 2.26e-09	0.00006*** 3.015e-07*** 3.035e-10***
j = 10	1st α_1 2nd α_2 3rd α_3	0.0002 –1.344e-06 9.866e-10	0.0003 8.85e-07 7.31e-10	0.00002*** 9.401e-08*** 8.532e-11***
Cooperation j = 1	1st α_1 2nd α_2 3rd α_3	–0.001 5.944e-06 –9.273e-09	0.0007 5.28e-06 1.07e-08	0.0008 5.780e-06 1.148e-08
j = 2	1st α_1 2nd α_2 3rd α_3	–0.0003 1.370e-06 –1.748e-09	0.0004 1.91e-06 2.13e-09	0.0005 2.077e-06 2.268e-09
j = 3	1st α_1 2nd α_2 3rd α_3	0.0003 –4.961e-07 1.316e-10	0.0002 4.28e-07 2.44e-10	0.0002 4.395e-07 2.541e-10
j = 4	1st α_1 2nd α_2 3rd α_3	0.0003 –8.299e-07 5.783e-10	0.0002 5.66e-07 4.16e-10	0.0002 6.064e-07 4.445e-10

(continued)

Table 2.8 (continued)

Distance	Order	OLS estimate	Robust S.E	Spatial S.E
j = 5	1st α_1 2nd α_2 3rd α_3	0.0001 –6.193e-07 3.596e-10	0.0003 8.00e-07 5.56e-10	0.0003 8.697e-07 6.006e-10
j = 6	1st α_1 2nd α_2 3rd α_3	-0.0005 7.575e-07 –3.168e-10	0.0003* 7.67e-07 6.14e-10	0.0003* 8.289e-07 6.428e-10
j = 7	1st α_1 2nd α_2 3rd α_3	0.0002 –7.786e-07 5.810e-10	0.0002 5.81e-07 4.25e-10	0.0002 6.309e-07 4.610e-10
j = 8	1st α_1 2nd α_2 3rd α_3	0.0001 –5.629e-07 4.428e-10	0.0002 5.61e-07 4.19e-10	0.0002 5.999e-07 4.498e-10
j = 9	1st α_1 2nd α_2 3rd α_3	–0.0007 1.528e-06 –1.165e-09	0.0005 2.22e-06 2.23e-09	0.0006 2.404e-06 2.366e-09
j = 10	1st α_1 2nd α_2 3rd α_3	0.0002 –1.315e-06 9.662e-10	0.0002 8.81e-07 7.28e-10	0.0002 8.972e-07 7.474e-10
Independence	1st α_1 2nd α_2 3rd α_3	–0.006 0.00008 –3.029e-07	0.001*** 0.00002*** 7.27e-08***	0.0003*** 5.350e-06*** 2.135e-08***

Note * refers to significance at 10%, ** at 5%, and *** at 1% level

correlated and correlation with productivity shocks is higher for labor than for capital stocks, an OLS estimate of a coefficient on labor input would be overestimated and that of a coefficient on capital stocks would be underestimated.

In order to address the simultaneity problem, we follow a partially-linear, semi-parametric model of Levinsohn and Petrin (2003) with the firm's intermediate inputs a proxy variable for unobservable productivity.[2] Since we assume that plants' location choices are predetermined, an economic distance term of productivity determinant can be separable from an unobservable technology component $\omega_i^{\sim d}$. In the estimation equation $\ln y_{it} = \beta_0 + \beta_k \ln k_{it-1} + \beta_l \ln l_{it} + \beta_m \ln m_{it} + \sum_{s=1}^{3} \alpha_s (d_{it})^s + \omega_i^{\sim d} + \eta_{it}$ at a period t augmented by a third-order polynomial in an exogenous distance-variable, we assume a demand function m_{it} of a firm i for intermediate inputs $\ln m_{it}$,

[2] A seminal paper in the literature, Olley and Pakes (1996) present an identification method of production function estimated, which is an application of a partially-linear, semi-parametric model of Robinson (1988). Olley and Pakes (1996) use investment variables as a proxy for correlation between production inputs and unobservable productivity. Levinsohn and Petrin (2003), however, point out practical uselessness of the method since the Olley and Pakes (1996) identification relies on the monotonic inverse relation between investment and productivity. In practice, there are many observations of investment variable with a zero value in whatever plant-level data. The zero values break the monotonic condition on which the identification of Olley and Pakes (1996) crucially depends.

Table 2.9 Cross-sectional dependence (2–2): raw materials

Distance	Order	OLS estimate	Robust S.E	Spatial S.E
General	1st α_1 2nd α_2 3rd α_3	–0.007 0.00009 –3.474e-07	0.002*** 0.00002*** 8.63e-08***	0.002*** 0.00003*** 1.016e-07***
Relationship j = 1	1st α_1 2nd α_2 3rd α_3	–0.001 4.658e-06 –5.342e-09	0.0008 6.14e-06 1.26e-08	0.00007*** 4.295e-07*** 7.847e-10***
j = 2	1st α_1 2nd α_2 3rd α_3	0.0003 –6.443e-07 –1.980e-10	0.0005 2.07e-06 2.23e-09	0.00003*** 1.487e-07*** 1.743e-10
j = 3	1st α_1 2nd α_2 3rd α_3	0.0006 –9.580e-07 2.823e-10	0.0003** 4.87e-07** 2.69e-10	0.00001*** 2.289e-08*** 1.391e-11***
j = 4	1st α_1 2nd α_2 3rd α_3	0.0005 –1.307e-06 8.865e-10	0.0003* 7.14e-07* 5.20e-10*	0.00001*** 3.232e-08*** 2.383e-11***
j = 5	1st α_1 2nd α_2 3rd α_3	0.0004 –1.655e-06 1.035e-09	0.0003 8.92e-07* 6.13e-10*	0.00002*** 6.397e-08*** 5.099e-11***
j = 6	1st α_1 2nd α_2 3rd α_3	–0.001 1.933e-06 –9.955e-10	0.0003*** 8.34e-07** 6.58e-10	0.00002*** 7.194e-08*** 6.460e-11***
j = 7	1st α_1 2nd α_2 3rd α_3	0.0005 –1.573e-06 1.118e-09	0.0003* 7.30e-07** 5.32e-10**	0.00002*** 3.495e-08*** 2.332e-11***
j = 8	1st α_1 2nd α_2 3rd α_3	0.0003 –1.160e-06 8.482e-10	0.0002 7.03e-07* 5.23e-10	0.00001*** 3.407e-08*** 2.476e-11***
j = 9	1st α_1 2nd α_2 3rd α_3	–0.001 3.561e-06 –2.748e-09	0.0006** 2.56e-06 2.53e-09	0.00007*** 3.675e-07*** 3.656e-10***
j = 10	1st α_1 2nd α_2 3rd α_3	0.0002 –1.548e-06 1.196e-09	0.0003 1.02e-06 8.08e-10	0.00003*** 1.157e-07*** 9.953e-11***
Cooperation j = 1	1st α_1 2nd α_2 3rd α_3	–0.001 5.906e-06 –7.437e-09	0.0008* 6.12e-06 1.26e-08	0.0008* 6.255e-06 1.299e-08
j = 2	1st α_1 2nd α_2 3rd α_3	0.0004 –8.511e-07 –1.778e-11	0.0005 2.04e-06 2.21e-09	0.0005 2.168e-06 2.328e-09
j = 3	1st α_1 2nd α_2 3rd α_3	0.0006 –9.581e-07 2.800e-10	0.0002** 4.81e-07** 2.67e-10	0.0002*** 4.860e-07** 2.798e-10
j = 4	1st α_1 2nd α_2 3rd α_3	0.0005 –1.344e-06 9.112e-10	0.0003* 7.09e-07* 5.17e-10*	0.0003* 7.203e-07* 5.316e-10*

(continued)

Table 2.9 (continued)

Distance	Order	OLS estimate	Robust S.E	Spatial S.E
j = 5	1st α_1	0.0004	0.0003	0.0004
	2nd α_2	–1.508e-06	9.02e-07*	9.410e-07
	3rd α_3	9.420e-10	6.17e-10	6.429e-10
j = 6	1st α_1	–0.001	0.0003***	0.0003***
	2nd α_2	1.929e-06	8.34e-07**	8.304e-07**
	3rd α_3	–9.931e-10	6.58e-10	6.564e-10
j = 7	1st α_1	0.0005	0.0003**	0.0003**
	2nd α_2	–1.639e-06	7.26e-07**	7.479e-07**
	3rd α_3	1.162e-09	5.30e-10**	5.507e-10**
j = 8	1st α_1	0.0003	0.0002	0.0002
	2nd α_2	–1.061e-06	7.06e-07	7.132e-07
	3rd α_3	7.944e-10	5.24e-10	5.384e-10
j = 9	1st α_1	–0.001	0.0006**	0.0006**
	2nd α_2	3.277e-06	2.52e-06	2.585e-06
	3rd α_3	–2.488e-09	2.50e-09	2.551e-09
j = 10	1st α_1	0.0001	0.0003	0.0003
	2nd α_2	–1.522e-06	1.01e-06	1.020e-06
	3rd α_3	1.176e-09	8.04e-10	8.180e-10
Independence	1st α_1	–0.008	0.002***	0.0004***
	2nd α_2	0.00009	0.00002***	6.961e-06***
	3rd α_3	–3.487e-07	8.55e-08***	2.775e-08***

Note * refers to significance at 10%, ** at 5%, and *** at 1% level

$$\ln m_{it} = m_{it}\left(\omega_{it}^{\sim d}, \ln k_{it-1}\right) \tag{2.9}$$

which proxies for productivity $\omega_i^{\sim d}$ at the current period and depends upon a state variable of capital stocks $\ln k_{it-1}$ at the end of the previous period t. It is also assumed that the demand function m_{it} is monotonic in the productivity $\omega_i^{\sim d}$ for all the capital stocks $\ln k_{it-1}$. The monotonicity of the intermediate inputs demand makes it possible to gain an inverse function $\omega_i^{\sim d} = \omega_i^{\sim d}(\ln m_{it}, \ln k_{it-1})$, which replaces the productivity term in the estimation equation:

$$\ln y_{it} = \beta_l \ln l_{it} + \sum_{s=1}^{3} \alpha_s (d_{it})^s + \phi_{it}(\ln m_{it}, \ln k_{it-1}) + \eta_{it} \tag{2.10}$$

where $\phi_{it}(\ln m_{it}, \ln k_{it-1}) \equiv \beta_0 + \beta_k \ln k_{it-1} + \beta_m \ln m_{it} + \omega_i^{\sim d}(\ln m_{it}, \ln k_{it-1})$. The monotonicity assumption leads to dropping from our data some samples with zero value of either material variable. The number of zero zero-value is 9 in the case of total materials or 48 for raw materials, in either 2002 or 2003.

The computational procedure is as follows. The first step of the Levinsohn and Petrin (2003) procedure with an application of a third-order polynomial $\sum_{p=0}^{3}\sum_{q=0}^{3-p}\delta_{pq}(\ln k_{it-1})^p(\ln m_{it})^q$ to the function $\phi_{it}(\ln m_{it}, \ln k_{it-1})$ is to consistently estimate a coefficient β_l on labour input $\ln l_{it}$ and coefficients α_s, $s = 1, 2$ and 3 on distance variables d_{it} in Eq. (2.10). Using the consistent estimates $\left(\widehat{\beta_l}, \widehat{\alpha_s}\right)$, $s = 1, 2$ and 3, the second step is to identify another coefficient (β_k, β_m) on capital stocks and intermediate inputs in Eq. (2.10). Using the estimates $\widehat{\phi_{it}}$ gained in the first step, we define $\widehat{\omega_i^{\sim d}} \equiv \widehat{\phi_{it}} - \beta_k \ln k_{it-1} - \beta_m \ln m_{it}$ for any value of (β_k, β_m). Assuming a first-order Markov process of productivity $\omega_i^{\sim d}$, we also define $\mathrm{E}(\widehat{\omega_{it}^{\sim d}|\omega_{it-1}^{\sim d}})$ as predicted values from a regression $\widehat{\omega_i^{\sim d}} = \gamma_0 + \gamma_0 \omega_i^{\sim d} + \gamma_0 \left(\omega_i^{\sim d}\right)^2 + \gamma_0 \left(\omega_i^{\sim d}\right)^2$. The residual for the estimation is

$$\widehat{\eta_{it} + \xi_{it}} = \ln y_{it} - \widehat{\beta_l} \ln l_{it} - \sum_{s=1}^{3} \widehat{\alpha_s} (d_{it})^s - \beta_k \ln k_{it-1} - \beta_m \ln m_{it} - \mathrm{E}(\widehat{\omega_{it}^{\sim d}|\omega_{it-1}^{\sim d}})$$

where an innovation to productivity $\xi_{it} \equiv \omega_{it}^{\sim d} - \mathrm{E}(\widehat{\omega_{it}^{\sim d}|\omega_{it-1}^{\sim d}})$. We use as instruments the first lagged capital stocks $\ln k_{it-2}$ and the first lag of the proxy variable $\ln m_{it-1}$. Two moment conditions $E(\eta_{it} + \xi_{it}|\ \ln k_{it-2})$ and $E(\eta_{it} + \xi_{it}|\ \ln m_{it-1})$ lead to just identified estimates $\left(\widehat{\beta_k}, \widehat{\beta_m}\right)$. Following Levinsohn and Petrin (2003), we use the Newton's method as a default solution to a minimization problem of the GMM criterion function, or when we obtain difficulties in convergence, we apply the grid search instead. The covariance matrix of the parameters is also calculated with the Stata's bootstrap command.

To examine whether the simultaneity problem affects the estimates gained in Sect. 2.3.2, we compare the GMM estimates with those from the Levinsohn and Petrin (2003) method. Estimation results without the productivity function are shown in Table 2.10 for total materials and in Table 2.11 for raw materials. The magnitude of the estimated coefficients totally changes, especially in the case of raw materials, where estimates of the coefficients on material and capital variables lose significance. The result suggests that without consideration of simultaneity between inputs, the OLS and GMM estimators generate overestimates of coefficients on labor inputs and underestimates of capital stocks coefficients in the production function. It implies the case where both production inputs are positively correlated, and correlation with productivity shocks is higher for labor than for capital stocks.

Estimations also reject a null of constant returns to scale, but once the simultaneity problem is considered, in the case of total materials, decreasing returns to scale emerge instead of increasing returns. The rejection of constant returns to scale is also confirmed in a case with value-added outputs as the dependent variable in the production function without any material input variable. The result leads to agglomeration, if any, brought about not by increasing returns to scale, but by productivity spillover among proximate suppliers around automobile assemblies.

Finally, we estimate the production function with productivity function using the Levinsohn and Petrin method. Results are shown in Table 2.12 for total materials and Table 2.13 for raw materials. The qualitative results are similar to the ones with cross-sectional dependence, especially in the case of raw materials. There are a lot of

Table 2.10 Simultaneity (1–1): Total materials

Variable (name)		Coefficients (Robust standard error)	
		GMM	LP
Labour (lnobe2)	β_l	0.52*** (0.03)	0.31*** (0.02)
Capital (lkstock2)	β_k	0.01** (0.005)	0.10** (0.04)
Materials (lmtotal2)	β_m	0.55*** (0.02)	0.08 (0.30)
Const	β_0	−1.52*** (0.22)	–
Returns to scale*		34.58(0)	3.78(0.05)
R^2		0.95	–
# of obs		2337	2337

Note x2 statistics and p-value in a parenthesis for constant returns-to-scale

Table 2.11 Simultaneity (1–2): Raw materials

Variable (name)		Coefficient (Robust standard error)	
		GMM	LP
Labour (lnobe2)	β_l	0.64*** (0.02)	0.40*** (0.02)
Capital (lkstock2)	β_k	0.03*** (0.006)	0.06 (0.04)
Materials (lzairyo2)	β_m	0.41*** (0.01)	0.12 (0.30)
Const	β_0	−1.71*** (0.21)	–
Returns to scale*		37.55(0)	0.65(0.42)
R^2		0.92	–
# of obs		2290	2306

Note x2 statistics and p-value in a parenthesis for constant returns-to-scale

congestion effects of type C-1, but we find robustly qualified agglomeration effects for some specific distances of general, relationship and cooperation $j = 1$ and$j = 6$, and independence in cases of raw materials. For a reference to the estimations, we plot the estimates of productivity, which is defined as a sum of the predicted productivity term $\widehat{E(\omega_{it}^{\sim d}|\omega_{it-1}^{\sim d})}$ and the economic distance term $\sum_{s=1}^{3} \widehat{\alpha_s}(d_{it})^s$ in the typical cases of cooperation distance for$j = 3$, probably with the congestion effect, and the general distance with the agglomeration effect, as is evident in Figs. 2.9 and 2.10, respectively.

Table 2.12 Simultaneity (2–1): total materials

Distance	Input			Distance			Returns to scale
	Labor	Capital	Materials	1st order	2nd	3rd	
General	0.31*** (0.02)	0.10** (0.04)	0.08 (0.31)	–0.0006 (0.0008)	0.00001 (0.00001)	–6.51e-08 (5.17e-08)	3.60 (0.06)
Relationship j = 1	0.31*** (0.02)	0.10** (0.04)	0.08 (0.28)	0.0005 (0.0005)	–4.44e-06 (3.48e-06)	7.99e-09 (7.26e-09)	3.90 (0.05)
j = 2	0.31*** (0.02)	0.10** (0.05)	0.08 (0.29)	–0.00008 (0.0003)	8.08e-07 (1.30e-06)	–1.26e-09 (1.59e-09)	4.12 (0.04)
j = 3	0.31*** (0.02)	0.10** (0.05)	0.08 (0.30)	0.0002 (0.0001)	–2.24e-07 (3.13e-07)	4.51e-11 (1.95e-10)	3.25 (0.07)
j = 4	0.31*** (0.02)	0.10** (0.04)	0.08 (0.30)	0.0004*** (0.0001)	–1.02e-06*** (3.93e-07)	7.02e-10** (2.91e-10)	3.38 (0.07)
j = 5	0.31*** (0.02)	0.10** (0.04)	0.08 (0.29)	–0.0002 (0.0002)	4.96e-07 (5.48e-07)	–3.81e-10 (4.09e-10)	2.81 (0.09)
j = 6	0.31*** (0.02)	0.10** (0.05)	0.08 (0.29)	–0.0003* (0.0002)	6.10e-07 (5.28e-07)	–4.02e-10 (4.59e-10)	4.02 (0.04)
j = 7	0.31*** (0.02)	0.10** (0.04)	0.08 (0.28)	0.0004*** (0.0001)	–1.01e-06*** (3.48e-07)	7.05e-10*** (2.58e-10)	4.86 (0.03)
j = 8	0.31*** (0.02)	0.10** (0.04)	0.08 (0.29)	0.0003*** (0.0001)	–8.97e-07** (3.58e-07)	6.37e-10** (2.69e-10)	3.80 (0.05)
j = 9	0.31*** (0.02)	0.10** (0.04)	0.08 (0.29)	0.00003 (0.0004)	–3.64e-07 (1.62e-06)	1.58e-10 (1.69e-09)	3.76 (0.05)
j = 10	0.31*** (0.02)	0.10** (0.05)	0.08 (0.30)	–0.0001 (0.0002)	3.27e-07 (6.63e-07)	–3.29e-10 (5.53e-10)	3.16 (0.08)
Cooperation j = 1	0.31*** (0.02)	0.10** (0.04)	0.08 (0.26)	0.0005 (0.0005)	–4.16e-06 (3.58e-06)	7.54e-09 (7.60e-09)	4.33 (0.04)
j = 2	0.31*** (0.02)	0.10** (0.05)	0.08 (0.30)	–0.00008 (0.0003)	8.11e-07 (1.30e-06)	–1.27e-09 (1.58e-09)	3.76 (0.05)
j = 3	0.31*** (0.02)	0.10** (0.04)	0.08 (0.31)	0.0001 (0.0002)	–2.17e-07 (3.29e-07)	4.19e-11 (2.00e-10)	3.37 (0.07)
j = 4	0.31*** (0.02)	0.10** (0.05)	0.08 (0.30)	0.0004*** (0.0001)	–1.04e-06*** (3.69e-07)	7.14e-10*** (2.73e-10)	3.22 (0.07)
j = 5	0.31*** (0.02)	0.10** (0.05)	0.08 (0.29)	–0.0002 (0.0002)	5.30e-07 (5.85e-07)	–4.01e-10 (4.38e-10)	3.18 (0.07)
j = 6	0.31*** (0.02)	0.10** (0.04)	0.08 (0.26)	–0.0003 (0.0002)	6.09e-07 (5.68e-07)	–4.01e-10 (4.92e-10)	4.60 (0.03)
j = 7	0.31*** (0.02)	0.10** (0.05)	0.08 (0.30)	0.0004*** (0.0001)	–1.01e-06** (3.98e-07)	7.09e-10** (2.94e-10)	3.53 (0.06)
j = 8	0.31*** (0.02)	0.10** (0.05)	0.08 (0.29)	0.0003** (0.0001)	–9.05e-07** (3.67e-07)	6.44e-10** (2.72e-10)	4.21 (0.04)
j = 9	0.31*** (0.02)	0.10** (0.05)	0.08 (0.29)	0.00007 (0.0003)	–5.24e-07 (1.67e-06)	3.01e-10 (1.79e-09)	3.26 (0.07)

(continued)

Table 2.12 (continued)

Distance	Input			Distance			Returns to scale
	Labor	Capital	Materials	1st order	2nd	3rd	
j = 10	0.31*** (0.02)	0.10** (0.05)	0.08 (0.33)	–0.0001 (0.0002)	3.37e-07 (6.44e-07)	–3.36e-10 (5.42e-10)	3.70 (0.05)
Independence	0.31*** (0.02)	0.10** (0.04)	0.08 (0.31)	–0.0006 (0.0008)	0.00001 (0.00001)	–6.53e-08 (5.30e-08)	4.61 (0.03)

2.5 Conclusion

This chapter, in the spirit of Marshall (1920) raised a question of how economic distance affects firm productivity, focusing on the distributions of productivity shared by auto-parts companies on the periphery of automobile assembly plants. We estimated the production functions of Japanese auto-parts plants, with special attention to the productivity function of measured economic distance. We considered the econometric issues of cross-sectional dependence of productivity and a simultaneity problem between inputs, as well as the standard OLS and GMM estimators.

It turned out that the number of membership companies with associations for technology cooperation is very limited. The rest of the auto-parts corporations are independent of the memberships. The general or independent plants gain positive technological externalities, which are robust to specifications of the production functions. The agglomeration effects are rarely observed for relation-specific or cooperative plants. Some of them cost the auto-parts plants or the member companies substantial negative externalities. Once the simultaneity problem is considered, decreasing returns to scale emerge instead of increasing returns. Material variables lose significance in the production functions. The rejection of constant returns to scale leads to agglomeration, if any, brought about not by increasing returns to scale, but by productivity spillover among proximate suppliers around automobile assemblies.

In future work, we hope to incorporate another econometric issue: the group effects on individual response variables in a cluster sample, following Wooldridge (2003).

Table 2.13 Simultaneity (2–2): raw materials

Distance	Input			Distance			Returns to scale
	Labor	Capital	Materials	1st order	2nd	3rd	
General	0.41*** (0.02)	0.06 (0.05)	0.12 (0.28)	–0.002** (0.001)	0.00003* (0.00001)	–1.15e-07** (5.49e-08)	0.72 (0.40)
Relationship j = 1	0.41*** (0.02)	0.06 (0.05)	0.12 (0.31)	–0.0009* (0.0005)	3.62e-06 (3.55e-06)	–5.82e-09 (6.70e-09)	0.64 (0.42)
j = 2	0.40*** (0.02)	0.06 (0.06)	0.12 (0.28)	0.0004 (0.0003)	–8.70e-07 (1.39e-06)	–6.17e-11 (1.61e-09)	0.51 (0.47)
j = 3	0.40*** (0.02)	0.06 (0.04)	0.13 (0.30)	0.0006*** (0.0002)	–8.00e-07** (3.29e-07)	2.17e-10 (1.86e-10)	0.48 (0.49)
j = 4	0.40*** (0.02)	0.06 (0.04)	0.13 (0.28)	0.0007*** (0.0002)	–1.99e-06*** (4.22e-07)	1.33e-09*** (2.96e-10)	0.56 (0.46)
j = 5	0.41*** (0.02)	0.06 (0.05)	0.12 (0.28)	–0.00005 (0.0002)	–2.51e-07 (6.06e-07)	1.08e-10 (4.43e-10)	0.52 (0.47)
j = 6	0.41*** (0.02)	0.06 (0.04)	0.13 (0.27)	–0.0007*** (0.0002)	1.04e-06* (5.65e-07)	–5.33e-10 (4.75e-10)	0.60 (0.44)
j = 7	0.40*** (0.02)	0.06 (0.04)	0.13 (0.29)	0.0007*** (0.0001)	–2.18e-06*** (4.11e-07)	1.49e-09*** (3.05e-10)	0.56 (0.45)
j = 8	0.40*** (0.02)	0.06 (0.05)	0.13 (0.28)	0.0006*** (0.0002)	–1.84e-06*** (4.09e-07)	1.27e-09*** (2.93e-10)	0.69 (0.41)
j = 9	0.41*** (0.02)	0.06 (0.04)	0.13 (0.31)	–0.0006* (0.0003)	4.57e-07 (1.51e-06)	–1.29e-10 (1.54e-09)	0.66 (0.42)
j = 10	0.41*** (0.02)	0.06 (0.05)	0.12 (0.31)	–0.0002 (0.0002)	1.63e-07 (7.16e-07)	–1.71e-10 (5.72e-10)	0.49 (0.48)
Cooperation j = 1	0.41*** (0.02)	0.06 (0.05)	0.12 (0.29)	–0.001* (0.0005)	3.84e-06 (3.65e-06)	–6.15e-09 (6.92e-09)	0.64 (0.42)
j = 2	0.40*** (0.02)	0.06 (0.05)	0.12 (0.28)	0.0004 (0.0003)	–7.83e-07 (1.39e-06)	–1.52e-10 (1.61e-09)	0.74 (0.39)
j = 3	0.40*** (0.02)	0.06 (0.04)	0.13 (0.25)	0.0005*** (0.0002)	–7.40e-07** (3.69e-07)	1.89e-10 (2.17e-10)	0.52 (0.47)
j = 4	0.40*** (0.02)	0.06 (0.05)	0.13 (0.30)	0.0007*** (0.0002)	–1.98e-06*** (4.49e-07)	1.32e-09*** (3.19e-10)	0.53 (0.47)
j = 5	0.41*** (0.02)	0.06 (0.04)	0.12 (0.28)	–0.0002 (0.0003)	1.26e-08 (6.64e-07)	–5.80e-11 (4.59e-10)	0.42 (0.52)
j = 6	0.41*** (0.02)	0.06 (0.04)	0.13 (0.29)	–0.0007*** (0.0002)	1.04e-06* (6.07e-07)	–5.32e-10 (5.02e-10)	0.51 (0.47)
j = 7	0.40*** (0.02)	0.06 (0.04)	0.13 (0.27)	0.0007*** (0.0002)	–2.16e-06*** (4.33e-07)	1.47e-09*** (3.09e-10)	0.56 (0.46)
j = 8	0.40*** (0.02)	0.06 (0.04)	0.13 (0.30)	0.0005*** (0.0002)	–1.62e-06*** (4.46e-07)	1.14e-09*** (3.22e-10)	0.62 (0.43)
j = 9	0.41*** (0.02)	0.06 (0.05)	0.13 (0.30)	–0.0005 (0.0004)	2.88e-07 (1.65e-06)	2.27e-11 (1.70e-09)	0.69 (0.41)

(continued)

Table 2.13 (continued)

Distance	Input			Distance			Returns to scale
	Labor	Capital	Materials	1st order	2nd	3rd	
j = 10	0.41*** (0.02)	0.06 (0.04)	0.12 (0.27)	–0.0003 (0.0002)	2.42e-07 (7.02e-07)	–2.27e-10 (5.72e-10)	0.45 (0.50)
Independence	0.41*** (0.02)	0.06 (0.04)	0.12 (0.31)	–0.002** (0.001)	0.00003* (0.00002)	–1.18e-07** (5.73e-08)	0.64 (0.42)

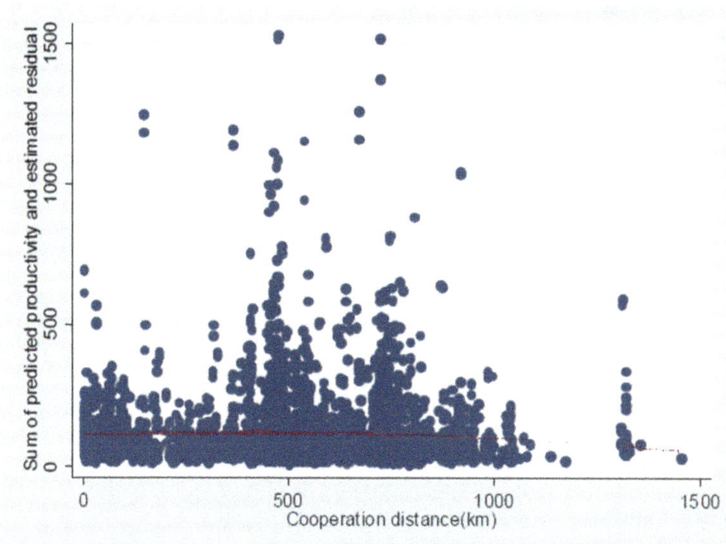

Fig. 2.9 Productivity estimates (cooperation distance, j = 3) with quadratic curvature

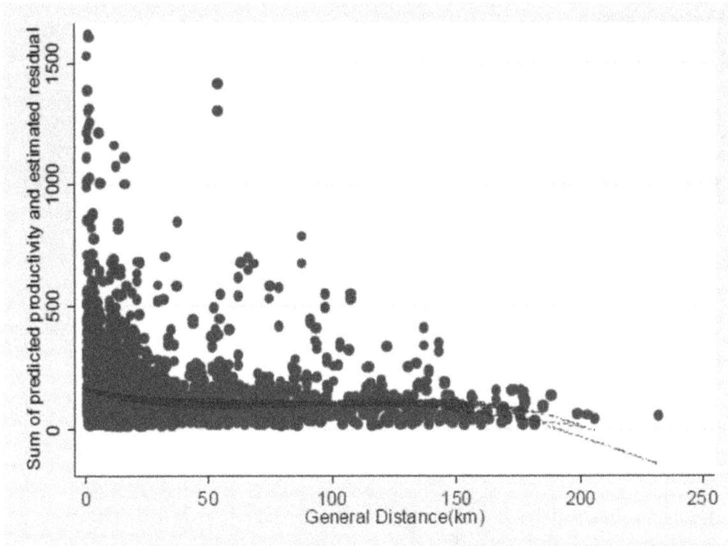

Fig. 2.10 Productivity estimate (general distance) with cubic curvature

Appendix: Variables Used and Their Construction

Summary statistics are indicated in Table 2.14.

A.2.1. Observations

The *Census of Manufactures*, conducted by the Ministry of Economy, Trade and Industry, Government of Japan, covers establishments or enterprises that produce manufactured goods and mineral products (including processed products) set forth by the ministerial ordinance. Survey items consist of minerals, steel and iron, non-ferrous metals, metal products, general machinery, electric machinery, transport machinery, precision machinery, ceramics, stone and clay products, manufactured chemical products, oil and coal products, plastics, pulp and paper, paper and paper-processed goods, manufactured textile products, rubber products, leather products, and other manufactured products.

We use cross-sectional data from the survey in fiscal year 2003, along with the year 2002 data as a supplemental sample in panel data. We confine the sample into plants with more than 30 employees. This chapter covers two items: automotive body and concomitant of a 4-digit industrial sub-classification 3012; and automotive component and accessory of a classification number 3013. We exclude automobiles (including two-wheeled vehicle) of classification 3011 since the automobile sector contains plants of motor corporations operating as a core system of the whole automobile industry, with probably different technologies than those acquired by the constructors of automotive parts belonging to the classifications 3012 and 3013. The year 2002 and 2003 data are matched with a STATA program identifying "firm

Table 2.14 Summary statistics (year 2003)

Variable	Name	# of obs	Unit	Mean	S.D	Min	Max	# of zero
Output	lpoutput2	2346	Ten thousand yen (ln, real)	12.46	1.44	9.01	17.99	0
Labor	lnobe2	2346	Man-hours (ln)	14.40	0.95	12.78	18.93	0
Capital	lkstock2	2346	Ten thousand yen (ln, real)	11.09	2.62	0	16.56	75
Materials	lmtotal2	2346	Ten thousand yen (ln, real)	11.70	1.95	0	17.73	9
	lzairyo2	2346	Ten thousand yen (ln, real)	11.16	2.56	0	17.72	40
Distance								
General	Ttdis	2346	Km	28.91	36.22	0	231.56	11
Relationship								
j = 1	tdis1	2346	Km	143.89	106.62	0	359.73	5
2	tdis2	2346	Km	180.83	124.15	0	775.29	2
3	tdis3	2346	Km	540.38	245.81	0.44	1454.53	0
4	tdis4	2346	Km	280.62	242.84	0	1116.71	1
5	tdis5	2346	Km	272.62	179.42	0.40	1193.00	0
6	tdis6	2346	Km	214.86	200.12	0	1105.54	1
7	tdis7	2346	Km	269.98	248.08	0.52	1117.14	0
8	tdis8	2346	Km	267.19	247.40	0.59	1112.02	0
9	tdis9	2346	Km	92.08	97.85	0	857.94	1
10	tdis10	2346	Km	174.41	160.31	0	1102.84	1
Cooperation								
j = 1	pdis1	2346	Km	143.49	106.80	0	359.73	19
2	pdis2	2346	Km	180.22	124.36	0	775.29	12
3	pdis3	2346	Km	538.22	247.64	0	1454.53	11
4	pdis4	2346	Km	279.85	243.28	0	1116.71	12
5	pdis5	2346	Km	272.14	179.87	0	1193.00	7
6	pdis6	2346	Km	214.86	200.13	0	1105.54	3
7	pdis7	2346	Km	269.40	248.36	0	1117.14	9

(continued)

Table 2.14 (continued)

Variable	Name	# of obs	Unit	Mean	S.D	Min	Max	# of zero
8	pdis8	2346	Km	266.19	247.65	0	1112.02	11
9	pdis9	2346	Km	91.59	98.07	0	857.94	20
10	pdis10	2346	Km	173.67	160.53	0	1102.84	14
Independence								
	pdis11	2346	Km	28.66	36.26	0	231.56	49

ID" distributed among the sample plants, which resulted in the sample of 2,346 observations.

The location on maps browsed with Google Earth is displayed separately in Fig. 2.1 for "cooperation" plants defined with a dummy variable $\text{dum}_j = 1$ for either $j = 1, \cdots, 10$ or in Fig. 2.2 for "independent" plants with a dummy $\text{dum}_{-j} = 1$. Construction of these dummy variables are described in a list of "cooperation distance" below.

A.2.2. Output

We construct nominal output as a sum of total shipment value, and the changes in manufactured products and semifinished goods in inventory at the beginning and the end of the year in the *Census of Manufactures*. The real term is the nominal values divided by industry organization (IO) deflators in the *Japan Industrial Productivity Database 2006* (JIP 2006 database available in http://www.rieti.go.jp/en/database/d05.html). The JIP database has been compiled in a collaboration between the Research Institute of Economy, Trade and Industry (RIETI) as a part of its research project, "Study on Industry-Level and Firm-Level Productivity in Japan," and the Hitotsubashi University as a part of its Hi-Stat (21st-Century COE Program, "Research Unit for Statistical Analysis in the Social Sciences") project. The original version of the JIP Database (ESRI/Hi-Stat JIP Database 2003) was compiled through a collaboration between the Economic and Social Research Institute (ESRI), Cabinet office, Government of Japan, as part of its research project on "Japan's Potential Growth," and the Hitotsubashi University Hi-Stat project.

JIP 2006 contains annual data on 108 sectors from 1970–2002, which can be used for total factor productivity (TFP) analyses. The database includes detailed information on sectoral capital service input indices and labor service input indices, including information on real capital stocks and the nominal cost of capital by type of capital and industry; annual nominal and real input–output tables; as well as some supplementary tables, such as statistics on trade, inward and outward FDI, and Japan's industrial structure. All real values are based on 1995 prices. The database is currently updated to 2008 and publicly available on a website.

A.2.3. Labor input

We construct labor input as a product of total number of full-time employees in the *Census of Manufactures* and industrial person-hours in the JIP2006 database.

A.2.4. Capital stock

We calculate the market values of tangible fixed assets by multiplying tangible fixed assets held at the beginning of the year in the *Census of Manufactures*, and the ratio of market to book values compiled in the JIP2006 database. Each plant i's market values kit at the beginning of year $t + 1$ are constructed following an equation

$$k_{it} = k_{it-1}(1 - \delta) + i_{it} \quad (2.12)$$

where δ is an annual industrial depreciation rate in the JIP2006 and i_{it} is the acquisition value of tangible fixed assets in the *Census of Manufactures*.

Note that the timing of our capital variable is different from that in Levinsohn and Petrin (2003), who "assume investment occurring in this period enters capital in this period." In contrast, not only this chapter, but also Olley and Pakes (1996) assume that "investment reported last period enters the production function as capital in this period." (p. 324, Levinsohn & Petrin, 2003).

A.2.5. Intermediate inputs or materials

We consider total materials, including raw materials, fuel, electricity and outsourcing costs, as well as raw materials used. The deflator is the IO deflators in the JIP2006 database.

A.2.6. Demand shifters

A.2.6.1. Product dummy

As variables controlling for demand effects in production functions, we include the product dummy variables, which are equal to 1 if plants list each product, or 0 otherwise. The products cover 28 items subordinate to the two broader classifications of auto parts (figures in bracket meaning the number of non-zero values): fabricated textile products, n.e.c., including knitted ones [3]; aluminum machinery parts, without machine finishing [2]; stamped and pressed machinery parts, without machine finishing [14]; piston rings [3]; starter generators [2]; miscellaneous auxiliary equipment for internal combustion engines [8]; parts, attachments and accessories of auxiliary equipment for internal combustion engines [13]; miscellaneous industrial electric machinery and apparatus [2]; passenger car bodies [18]; bus bodies [10]; truck bodies [71]; special-use car bodies [47]; trailers, including trailer chassis and bodies [13]; auto-body and concomitance [14]; gasoline engines for motor vehicles [18]; diesel engines for motor vehicles [10]; internal combustion engines for motorcycles and motor scooters [3]; parts, attachments and accessories of internal combustion engines for motor vehicles [500]; parts of driving, transmission and operating units [507]; parts of suspension and brake systems [273]; parts of chassis and bodies [480]; car air-conditioners [57]; car heaters [7]; finished seats [51]; miscellaneous parts of motor vehicles, including parts of motorcycles [686]; KD sets (passenger cars, buses and trucks) [2]; KD sets (motorcycles) [3]; and auto-components and accessories [431].

A.2.6.2. Products Share

As a proxy for the pricing power held by each plant, we use product share variables, defined as product shares of a plant's shipment value to total shipment values summed over the sample plants. The share variables also involve the same 28 product items as the product dummy variables. If the auto-parts supplier does not list the products, the variables are equal to 0. The number of non-zero values for the product share variables is also the same as that of the product dummy variables.

A.2.6.3. Products Inventory

According to the production smoothing hypothesis, the inventory ratios would be chosen by plants to smoothen production in the face of a large variance in product demand. The product inventory variables are defined as ratios of a plant's inventory to shipment values of manufactured products. If suppliers do not manufacture the products, the variables are equal to 0. Excluding the products with all the values 0, we use 20 product items, less than the number of product dummy and share variables.

The products are fabricated textile products, n.e.c., including knitted ones [3]; miscellaneous auxiliary equipment for internal combustion engines [8]; parts, attachments and accessories of auxiliary equipment for internal combustion engines [12]; passenger car bodies [9]; truck bodies [30]; special-use car bodies [11]; trailers, including trailer chassis and bodies [7]; gasoline engines for motor vehicles [11]; diesel engines for motor vehicles [5]; internal combustion engines for motorcycles and motor scooters [2]; parts, attachments, and accessories of internal combustion engines for motor vehicles [430]; parts of driving, transmission, and operating units [439]; parts of suspension and brake systems [248]; parts of chassis and bodies [421]; car air-conditioners [49]; car heaters [4]; finished seats [43]; and miscellaneous parts of motor vehicles, including parts of motorcycles [567].

A.2.7. Economic distance

A.2.7.1. General economic distance

As described in Sect. 2.2.2, we construct three types of economic distance measures: general; relationship; cooperation; or independence. In making these measures, we need to transform the address information of each plant listed in the *Census of Manufactures* into latitude and longitude. On the basis of the lat/long information, we use the ArcGIS software to calculate minimum distance d_i^g of plant i from any automobile construction plant affiliated with 10 major motor corporations. The distance measure is "general," that is, technology is potentially accessible for any plant located within a sphere of another plant.

A.2.7.2. Relationship distance

We also measure another distance of plants from any core plant of the motor corporations: Daihatsu (head office, Ikeda, Kyoto, and Shiga plants, or machinery engineering division (Tada plant)); Hino (head office and Hino, Hamura, or Nitta plants); Honda (Saitama, Suzuka, Kumamoto, Hamamatsu, or Tochigi plants); Isuzu (Tochigi or Fujisawa plants); Matsuda (plant complex in the head office and Ujina district, and Miyoshi and Hofu plants (Nishinoura and Nakanoseki districts)); Mitsubishi (Okazaki, Kyoto, Shiga, and Mizushima plants, or Pajero Manufacturing Co. Ltd.);

Nissan (Tochigi, Oppama, Kyushu, Nissan Body Shonan, Yokohama, or Iwaki plants); Subaru (Gunma Main, Gunma Yajima, Gunma Ota North, Gunma Oizumi, or Isesaki plants); Suzuki (head office, and Takatsuka, Iwata, Osuka, Kosai, or Sagara plants), and Toyota (head plant, Motomachi, Kamigo, Takaoka, Miyoshi, Tsutsumi, Myochi, Shimoyama, Kinuura, Tahara, Teiho, or Hirose plants, Toyota Motor Hokkaido Inc., or Toyota Motor Tohoku Co. Ltd.). The measure $d_{i,j}^{r}$ for a plant i and a motor corporation j is called the "relationship" distance since technology is accessible for plants establishing transactional relationships with either motor assembly company.

A.2.7.3. Cooperation Distance

The third measure of economic distance is the "cooperation" distance $d_{i,j}^{c}$, since we focus on the membership with associations for technological cooperation affilated with the 10 major motor assembly corporations. According to the *Japanese Auto Parts Industries* (Japan Auto Parts Industries Association), there are some associations for technological cooperation affilated with the major assembly companies: Daihatsu Kyoyu-kai; Hino Kyoryoku-kai; Isuzu Kyowa-kai; Nishi-Nihon Youko-kai, Kanto Youko-kai, and Kansai Youko-kai (all for Matsuda Motor Corporation); Nissho-kai (for Nissan); Subaru Yuhi-kai; Suzuki Kyoryoku-kyodo-kumiai; and Kyoho-kai (for Toyota). A representative association of Toyota, Kyoho-kai, says on the website,

> The objective of KYOHOKAI is, together with Toyota Motor Corporation and its member companies, to make world economic and social contributions through activities based upon a global and open partnership. To aim for further sharing of information and the enhancement of 2-way communication with Toyota Motor Corporation based on the policy of Toyota Motor Corporation to "create solid footing and build a stronger foundation." The member companies shall develop meeting activities for the purpose of mutual study and exchange to strengthen our global competitive edge and to continue growth by focusing on the "Pursuit of quality." To further enhance and improve the efficiency of meeting activities.

In year 2003's sample, the number of member companies is very limited, as is evident from the number of zero values shown in the summary statistics of Table 2.14. In addition to the member companies of the associations, the *Japanese Auto Parts Industries* contain information on the business partners of Honda Motor Co. and Mitsubishi Motors Co. We construct 10 dummy variables dum_j, $j = 1, \cdots, 10$ for each plant that take a value of 1 if it is a member company, or 0 otherwise. Product terms of the dummy variable $1-\text{dum}_j$ and the relationship distance $d_{i,j}^{r}$ indicate shared technological knowledge among the members of the association for technological cooperation; so we call the distance "cooperation through relationship."

A.2.7.4. Independence distance

We also construct the other dummy variable dum_{-j} representing no membership of the 10 major assembly corporations. Product term of the independence dummy dum_{-j} and the general distance dum_i is a distance measure d_i^{i} for independent companies. The independent companies make up the majority of the 2003 sample shown in Table 2.14.

References

Bond, S. & Soderbom, M. (2005). Adjustment costs and the identification of Cobb Douglas production functions. Economics Papers. Economics Group, Nuffield College, University of Oxford.

Conley, T. G. (1999). GMM estimation with cross sectional dependence. *Journal of Econometrics, 92*(1), 1–45.

Conley, T. G., & Ligon, E. (2002). Economic distance and cross-country spillover. *Journal of Economic Growth, 7*(2), 157–187.

Davidson, R., & MacKinnon, J. G. (2003). *Econometric theory and methods.* Oxford University Press.

Griliches, Z., & Mairesse, J. (1998). Production functions: The search for identification. *Econometrics and economic theory in the twentieth century: The Ragnar Frisch centennial symposium* (pp. 169–203). Cambridge University Press.

Hidalgo, C. (2015). *Why information grows: The evolution of order, from atoms to economies.* Basic Books.

Levinsohn, J., & Petrin, A. (2003). Estimating production functions using inputs to control for unobservables. *Review of Economic Studies, 70*(2), 317–341.

Manski, C. F. (1993). Identification of endogenous social effects: The reflection problem. *The Review of Economic Studies, 60*(3), 531–542.

Marschak, J., & Andrews, W. H. (1944). Random simultaneous equations and the theory of production. *Econometrica, 12*(3/4), 143–205.

Marshall, A. (1920). *Principles of economics.* MacMillan.

Moulton, B. R. (1990). An illustration of a pitfall in estimating the effects of aggregate variables on micro units. *The Review of Economics and Statistics, 72*(2), 334–338.

Newey, W. K., & West, K. D. (1987). A simple, positive semi-definite, heteroskedasticity and autocorrelation consistent covariance matrix. *Econometrica, 55*(3), 703–708.

Olley, G. S., & Pakes, A. (1996). The dynamics of productivity in the telecommunications equipment industry. *Econometrica, 64*(6), 1263–1297.

Robinson, P. M. (1988). Root-N-consistent semiparametric regression. *Econometrica, 56*(4), 931–954.

Saxenian, A. (1996). *Regional advantage: Culture and competition in Silicon Valley and Route 128.* Harvard University Press.

Scitovsky, T. (1954). Two concepts of external economies. *Journal of Political Economy, 62*(2), 143–151.

Topkis, D. M. (1995). Comparative statics of the firm. *Journal of Economic Theory, 67*(2), 370–401.

White, H., & Domowitz, I. (1984). Nonlinear regression with dependent observations. *Econometrica, 52*(1), 143–161.

Wooldridge, J. M. (2003). Cluster-sample methods in applied econometrics. *American Economic Review Papers and Proceedings, 93*(2), 133–138.

Chapter 3
Initiative for Relation-Specific Skills

Contents

Abstract We conducted an empirical analysis on the hypothesis raised by (Asanuma, Journal of the Japanese & International Economies 3:1–30, 1989; Asanuma, B. (1992). Japanese manufacturer-supplier relationships in international perspective. In P. Sheard (Ed.), International adjustment and the Japanese economy. St. Leonards, Australia: Allen & Unwin, 99–124) on auto-parts procurement in Japan. The hypothesis proposes a new classification for auto-parts makers as per their degree of initiative in product and process design. The initiative results in "relation-specific skills" acquired by the sub-contractors in relation to auto manufacturers in the first tier. Among the responses to the hypothesis, (Milgrom and Roberts, Economics, organization & management, Prentice Hall, 1992) and (Holmström and Roberts, Journal of Economic Perspectives 12:73–94, 1998) focused on a role of the supplier association in the Japanese hierarchy system, where communication among suppliers

☆This chapter is based on Takeda and Uchida "Make or Buy, and/or Cooperate? The Property Rights Approach to Auto Parts Procurement in Japan," RIETI Discussion Paper Series 13-E-066, which was conducted as a part of the Research Institute of Economy, Trade and Industry (RIETI) research project, "Determinants of the Productivity Gap among Firms in Japan." We are grateful to RIETI for providing us with data and some data-converters, and the great opportunity to discuss our research; to Iichiro Uesugi for informing us of the availability of TSR data; to three interviewees at DENSO CORPORATION for giving us local inputs; to Tsukasa Uchida for arranging the interview; to participants in the 62nd Meeting of AFSE at Aix-en-Provence, France; to Keiichiro Oda for helpful comments; and to Yuki Kimura and Iori Sawai for excellent research assistance.

Y. Takeda and I. Uchida, *Information Agglomeration of Japanese Auto Parts Suppliers*,
https://doi.org/10.1007/978-981-19-3300-4_3

alleviates opportunistic misbehavior by automakers. This chapter, instead of the reputational role of the association, takes an alternative stand on the technology cooperation association from the property rights theory, especially a general setup of (Whinston, Journal of Law, Economics, & Organization 19:1–23, 2003). Participation in the associations should be considered as non-contractible investments for the relation-specific skill. The empirical implications of some specified models concern the effects on the vertical integration likelihood of the importance of both buyers' or sellers' non-contractible investments and specificity in the acquired relation-specific skills. We estimate an equation of vertical integration wherein the determinants are dummy variables of the parent firm and the subsidiary's participation in the cooperation associations, and variables representing the degree of their relation specificity. The significance and signs of these variables suggest that other than a model of exogenous acquisition of relation-specific skills, a model can also be applicable to Japanese auto parts supplier-manufacturers, where it is not the manufacturers' but the suppliers' investments that create their own relation-specific skills through association activities. The Asanuma hypothesis turns out to be alive.

Keyword Property rights approach; vertical integration; technology cooperation

3.1 Introduction

The chapter considers a role of initiative for relation-specific skills in lowering transaction costs associated with organizational links for information agglomeration, as introduced in Chap. 1 and Hidalgo (2015). Our specific interest is in the Asanuma hypothesis emphasizing a role of "relation-specific skills" in the Japanese auto-parts industry. The auto-parts suppliers probably have initiatives to acquire relation-specific skills via joining the technological cooperation associations.

To explore the empirical analysis, we rely upon a general setup of Whinston (2003), where non-contractible investments by a buyer or seller create the relation-specific skills. The comparative statics is conducted with respect to the effects on the integration likelihood of changes in the parameters pertinent to the importance of the relation-specific skill or specificity of the skill. In a comparison with the qualitative implications, we estimate, via Tobit and regressions of censored data on endogenous regressors (IV Tobit and special regressor probit (Lewbel et al., 2012)), a single equation of vertical integration with the determinants of that importance and specificity.

Does the Asanuma hypothesis hit the nail on the head? Which type of the property right model fits the Japanese auto-parts suppliers? Are there any positive roles of the associations for knowledge sharing in "the hold-up problem?" Yes, the Asanuma hypothesis turns out to be true. The model of exogenous acquisition of relation-specific skill or the model of a seller's self-investment for the relation-specific skill would be applicable to auto-parts procurement in Japan. Some associations may find it a place to make non-contractible investments, while others may not. As Asanuma (1989, 1992) once insisted, the Japanese auto-parts industry is still diversity-carrying.

The structure of the chapter is as follows: Sect. 3.2 reconsiders the Asanuma hypothesis; Sect. 3.3 explicates the property right approach to the hold-up problem; Sect. 3.4 estimates the likelihood of vertical integration via Tobit, IV Tobit, or special regressor probit models for comparison with the comparative statics; and finally, Sect. 3.5 concludes the discussion.

3.2 The Asanuma Hypothesis Revisited

Asanuma (1989, 1992), based on numerous discussions with businesspersons, made a hypothesis on subcontractors in the Japanese auto industry. He disaggregated the classical dichotomy of parts and suppliers, either drawings supplied (DS abbreviated; *taiyozu*, in Japanese) or drawings approved (DA; *shoninzu*) into a new classification according to the degree of initiative in design of the product and process.

There are three different categories in the DS parts: I. the core firm provides minute instructions for the manufacturing process; II. the supplier designs the manufacturing process based on the blueprints of products provided by the core firm; III. the core firm provides only the rough drawings, and their completion is entrusted to the supplier. Lowering the priority of the core firm's initiative on the list, the DA parts are divided into other three taxonomies: IV. the core firm provides the specifications and has substantial knowledge of the manufacturing process; V. the intermediate region between IV and VI; VI. although the core firm issues the specifications, it only has limited knowledge concerning the process. Finally, subordinate to the DA parts, the marketed goods are ranked seventh: VII. the core firm selects from a catalog offered by the supplier.

The close relation between the core firms and parts' suppliers, as the initiative classification suggests, fosters on the suppliers' side "relation-specific skills" classified into four categories: X1. capabilities that become visible through interactions held during the early development stage; X2. capabilities that become visible through interactions held during the late development stage; X3. capabilities that become visible at deliveries during the production stage; and X4. capabilities that become visible at price renegotiations during the production stage. Asanuma (1989) also shows the rigid relation of each core firm to a small number of member suppliers belonging to the associations for technology cooperation.

The Asanuma hypothesis on the relation-specific skills in the Japanese auto-parts industry once drew significant attention from the international community. Among the responses to the hypothesis, Milgrom and Roberts (1992) and Holmström and Roberts (1998) focused on a role of the supplier association in the Japanese hierarchy system, saying.

> Perhaps the major problem in the system may be that the automakers are inherently too powerful and thus face too great a temptation to misbehave opportunistically. . . . One counterbalance to this power asymmetry is the supplier association, which facilitates communication among the suppliers and ensures that if the auto company exploits its power over one, all will know and its reputation will be damaged generally. This raises the cost of misbehavior." (p.82, Holmström & Roberts, 1998)

What happens to the specific relation in the Japanese auto-parts industry? Can the Asanuma hypothesis still apply as convincingly as when Milgrom and Roberts raised it? Especially, do the supplier associations for technology cooperation play a substantive role in the formation of relation-specific skills? These questions are reminiscent of the classical Coasian issues of the firm's boundaries, in terms of which the Japanese auto-part suppliers still seem to lie in a gray zone. To answer the questions, the contemporary property-right approach to the firm's boundaries (Hart, 1995) should be considered. More concretely, instead of the Milgrom and Roberts view on relation-specific skills, this chapter considers that those skills might require "non-contractible investment," which is executed either by both manufacturers and suppliers, or one of them. The returns to non-contractible investment are considered as accruing through the interactions among suppliers joining the technology cooperation associations.

3.3 The Property Right Approach

As explained in Section 1.2.2 of Chap. 1, there are difficulties in empirically testing the property-right theory (PRT) to a firm's investment hold-up (Lafontaine & Slade, 2013). This chapter overcomes the difficulties both by drawing upon a general setup of Whinston (2003) for the pure property-right approach and by extracting information from "a natural experiment" of participation of suppliers in the auto-parts associations for technology cooperation.

3.3.1 A General Setup of Whinston (2003)

We consider a general setup of a bilateral trade between buyer B and seller S. The seller S uses an upstream asset for production. Though there is seller integration or joint ownership possible in principle, we confine the possible ownership form to buyer integration[1], where buyer B owns the upstream asset. We denote the ownership state by A_B. If buyer B owns the asset, then $A_B = 1$ where vertical integration occurs. When seller S owns it, there is non-integration $A_B = 0$.

---

[1] The Tokyo Shoko Research, LTD. (TSR) data indicate quite a low probability of the upstream seller's integrations, relative to that of the buyer integration in Japan. The parent company's ownership ratio of a subsidiary is on an average around 45% since 2000, while the subsidiary's ownership ratio of a parent company is on an average around 4%.

The timing of the setup is as follows. At time 0, the two parties decide who will own the asset and also agree on some "contractible" investments without any choice for the parties. The returns to the contractible investments are regarded as accruing in constant terms independent of the levels of "non-contractible" investments both in profits available from a bilateral trade between the parties and in payoffs to the parties in their next-best alternative to trading with each other. At time 1 then, each of the parties make "non-contractible investments" i_B and i_S, which are associated with costs $c_B(i_B)$ and $c_S(i_S)$, respectively. Finally at time 2, they do "Nash" bargaining over trade, assuming to have equal bargaining power and splitting any available surplus in half. For buyer B when $A_B = 0$, the alternative to bilateral trade with seller S is either to procure from another supplier, or shut down. When $A_B = 1$, buyer B might either procure the part from another supplier, hiring another manager to produce the input using the upstream asset owned by B, or shut down. Likewise, for seller S when $A_B = 0$, the alternative to trading with B is either to sell the product to another buyer, or shut down. When $A_B = 1$, seller S might either sell the part to another buyer using a technology without the asset owned by B, or shut down.

The profits from the bilateral trade of the buyer and seller $\pi(i_B, i_S)$ and the disagreement payoffs to each of them $\omega_B(i_B, i_S|A_B)$ and $\omega_S(i_B, i_S|A_B)$ are assumed to be expressed in such linear functional forms as follows: profits from the efficient trade with each other

$$\pi(i_B, i_S) = \alpha_0 + \alpha_B i_B + \alpha_S i_S;$$

payoffs to buyer B in his next-best alternative to trading with S (B's disagreement payoffs)

$$\omega_B(i_B, i_S|A_B) = (\beta_0 + \beta_{B0} i_B + \beta_{S0} i_S)(1 - A_B) + (\beta_1 + \beta_{B1} i_B + \beta_{S1} i_S)A_B;$$

payoffs to the seller in his next-best alternative to trading with B (S's disagreement payoffs)

$$\omega_S(i_B, i_S|A_B) = (\sigma_0 + \sigma_{S0} i_S + \sigma_{B0} i_B)(1 - A_B) + (\sigma_1 + \sigma_{S1} i_S + \sigma_{B1} i_B)A_B.$$

The cost functions are quadratic for simplicity: $c_B(i_B) = 0.5(i_B)^2$ and $c_S(i_S) = 0.5(i_S)^2$. We assume that parameter values satisfy the inequalities $\alpha_0 \geq \max\{\beta_0 + \sigma_0, \beta_1 + \sigma_1\}$, $\alpha_B \geq \max\{\beta_{B0} + \sigma_{B0}, \beta_{B1} + \sigma_{B1}\}$, and $\alpha_S \geq \max\{\beta_{S0} + \sigma_{S0}, \beta_{S1} + \sigma_{S1}\}$. These equations ensure that regardless of who owns the upstream asset, it is ex-post efficient for the parties to trade with each other. The ex-post efficiency sets off the hold-up problem.

This is very important in testing PRT, especially the assessment of the Asanuma hypothesis where participation in supplier associations plays a role in acquiring relation-specific skills, since we allow "cross-investments" in the disagreement payoffs as well as "self-investments". For instance, S might invest in training B on how to produce more efficiently, or S might invest in raising the quality of the goods produced with the upstream asset. In the first scenario, the physical capital i_S invested by S matters a great deal for B's disagreement payoffω_B. In the second, the efforts i_S made by S for the quality improvements would not only affect S's own disagreement payoffω_S, but also B's disagreement payoff ω_B if B owns the asset. According to the Asanuma hypothesis described above, those cross-investments are likely to exemplify suppliers' cooperative activities with manufacturers in the technology cooperation associations. Note that a setup of Hart (1995) is a restricted case without any cross-investments$\beta_{S0} = \beta_{S1} = \sigma_{B0} = \sigma_{B1} = 0$, in addition to $\alpha_B > \beta_{B1} > \beta_{B0} \geq 0$ and$\alpha_S > \sigma_{S0} > \sigma_{S1} \geq 0$.

3.3.1.1 The First-Best Investments

First, we find the first-best solution to the investment decisions of each party. The efficient levels of the investments $\left(i_B^{**}, i_S^{**}\right)$ are

$$\mathbf{argmax}\,\pi(\boldsymbol{i_B}, \boldsymbol{i_S}) - \boldsymbol{c_B}(\boldsymbol{i_B}) - \boldsymbol{c_S}(\boldsymbol{i_S}) \tag{3.1}$$

where the solution $\left(i_B^{**}, i_S^{**}\right) = (\alpha_B, \alpha_S)$. Then the decisions result in a joint surplus $W^{**} = \alpha_0 + 0.5(\alpha_B)^2 + 0.5(\alpha_S)^2$, to be split equally.

3.3.1.2 The Second-Best Investments and Integration Likelihood

We next consider equilibrium levels of the investments $\left(i_B^*, i_S^*\right)$ given the ownership $A_B = 0 \text{or} 1$. The buyer B maximizes

$$\omega_B(i_B, i_S|A_B) + 0.5[\pi(i_B, i_S) - \omega_B(i_B, i_S|A_B) - \omega_S(i_B, i_S|A_B)] - c_B(i_B),$$

where the second term means half of the quasi-rent received in the Nash bargaining between the buyer and seller. The solution is

$$\boldsymbol{i_B^*} = 0.5[\boldsymbol{\alpha_B} + (\boldsymbol{\beta_{B0}} - \boldsymbol{\sigma_{B0}})(1 - \boldsymbol{A_B}) + \left(\boldsymbol{\beta_{B1}} - \boldsymbol{\sigma_{B1}}\right)\boldsymbol{A_B}\big]. \tag{3.2}$$

Similarly, a decision of seller S given the ownership A_B is

$$\boldsymbol{i_S^*} = 0.5[\boldsymbol{\alpha_S} + \left(\boldsymbol{\sigma_{S0}} - \boldsymbol{\beta_{S0}}\right)(1 - \boldsymbol{A_B}) + \left(\boldsymbol{\sigma_{S1}} - \boldsymbol{\beta_{S1}}\right)\boldsymbol{A_B}\big]. \tag{3.3}$$

The equilibrium welfare level $W^*(A_B; \alpha, \beta, \sigma)$ is obtained by substituting the second-best investments Eqs. (3.2) and (3.3) with Eq. (3.1).

Now, we undertake some comparative statics analyses of how the changes in parameters affect the likelihood of vertical integration. The likelihood is determined by a difference in the welfare levels between the ownership structures $A_B = 0 \text{or} 1 : \Delta =$

$[W^*(A_B = 1; \alpha, \beta, \sigma) - W^*(A_B = 0; \alpha, \beta, \sigma)]$. A positive change in the equilibrium welfare level increases a likelihood of vertical integration.

First, the changes in parameters $(\alpha_0, \beta_0, \beta_1, \sigma_0, \sigma_1)$ are irrelevant to the welfare level changes, so they are "contractible" investments. Second, we move to changes in the marginal returns to non-contractible investments. Partial derivatives of the difference Δ with respect to each parameter show the following results:

$$\frac{\partial \Delta}{\partial \alpha_B} = 0.5\left[i_B^*(1; \bullet) - i_B^*(0; \bullet)\right],$$

where positive if B more invests under $A_B = 1$ than $A_B = 0$;

$$\frac{\partial \Delta}{\partial \alpha_S} = 0.5\left[i_S^*(1; \bullet) - i_S^*(0; \bullet)\right],$$

where negative if S more invests under $A_B = 0$ than $A_B = 1$;

$$\frac{\partial \Delta}{\partial \beta_{B0}} = -\frac{\partial \Delta}{\partial \sigma_{B0}} = -0.5\left[\alpha_B - i_B^*(0; \bullet)\right],$$

where negative if B underinvests under $A_B = 0$ relative to the first-best investment;

$$\frac{\partial \Delta}{\partial \beta_{B1}} = -\frac{\partial \Delta}{\partial \sigma_{B1}} = 0.5\left[\alpha_B - i_B^*(1; \bullet)\right],$$

where positive if B underinvests under $A_B = 1$ relative to the first best;

$$\frac{\partial \Delta}{\partial \sigma_{S0}} = -\frac{\partial \Delta}{\partial \beta_{S0}} = -0.5\left[\alpha_S - i_S^*(0; \bullet)\right],$$

where negative if S underinvests under $A_B = 0$ relative to the first best;

$$\frac{\partial \Delta}{\partial \sigma_{S1}} = -\frac{\partial \Delta}{\partial \beta_{S1}} = 0.5\left[\alpha_S - i_S^*(1; \bullet)\right],$$

where positive if S underinvests under $A_B = 1$ relative to the first best.

Note that it is apparent that these signs of partial derivatives crucially depend on whether to further invest under the ownership of the asset, and whether to divest relative to the first-best investment. If B (or S, in parallel) further invests under integration (non-integration) $A_B = 1$ $(A_B = 0)$, an increase in $\alpha_B(\alpha_S)$ increases the joint return from B's (S's) investment, resulting in a higher (lower) probability of integration. Further, in a divestment case, an increase in investment levels under an ownership structure raises the surplus generated under that structure. Those two conditions are in turn dependent on specific models of the Asanuma hypothesis describing whose non-contractible investments create the relation-specific skill for seller S, as will be explained later.

3.3.1.3 Theoretical Implications

It would be convenient for us to summarize some theoretical implications from the comparative statics of Whinston (2003)'s general setup. Broadly classified, the comparative statics is two-fold, with respect to either importance or specificity of the non-contractible investment.

The importance of B's investment in improving the upstream asset raises α_B, β_{B1}, andσ_{B0}, implying increases in marginal returns to B's non-contractible investment i_B. With divestment and further investment under a self-ownership, these parameter changes have the effect of increasing the integration likelihood. Likewise, the importance of S's investment in improving the asset raises α_S, β_{S1}, andσ_{S0}, that is, increases in marginal returns to S's non-contractible investmenti_S. The changes would reduce the integration likelihood, under the same conditions as above.

As for specificity, there are two types of marginal specificity: marginal people specificity for B of i_B indicated by a difference$\alpha_B - \beta_{B1}$; and marginal asset specificity for B of i_B measured by a difference$\beta_{B1} - \beta_{B0}$. The marginal people specificity for B is the amount by which marginal return to investment i_B is reduced when B has the asset ownership but does not deal with S. The marginal asset specificity for B is the amount by which marginal return to B's investment is further reduced without the asset ownership. An increase in the marginal people specificity, holding the marginal asset specificity fixed, is represented as equal-sized reductions in$\beta_{B1}$and β_{B0}, while an increase in the marginal asset specificity holding the people specificity fixed is shown as a decrease inβ_{B0}. Likewise, the marginal people specificity for S of i_S is measured by a difference$\alpha_S - \sigma_{S0}$, while the marginal asset specificity is measured by a difference$\sigma_{S0} - \sigma_{S1}$. An increase in the marginal people specificity, holding the marginal asset specificity fixed, is represented as equal-sized reductions inσ_{S0} and σ_{S1}, while an increase in the marginal asset specificity holding the people specificity fixed, is shown as a decrease inσ_{S0}.

3.3.2 Some Specific Models for the Asanuma Hypothesis

For an empirical analysis on the comparative statics in the general setup above, we construct some specific models applicable to the Asanuma hypothesis, each of which has a difference in "the degree of initiative in design of the product and the process," that is, whose non-contractible investments create relation-specific skills for seller S. The non-contractible investment also involves a participation in the cooperative activities among suppliers joining the technology cooperation associations.

We have three empirical questions: (1) does the Asanuma hypothesis hit the nail on the head?; (2) which type of the PRT model fits Japanese auto-parts suppliers?; (3) are there any positive roles of the associations for knowledge sharing in "the hold-up problem?" Each of the simplified models constructed below provide differential implications from the comparative statics with respect to the effects of both the importance and specificity on integration likelihood; the qualitative results will be tested using the Japanese auto-parts firms data in Sect. 3.3.

3.3.2.1 Model 1: Exogenous Relation-Specific Skill

Suppose that the "relation-specific skill" is exogenously given and B makes non-contractible self-investment complementary to S's acquisition of the skill. For the purpose, it is assumed that only B has a non-contractible investment, and that$\sigma_{B0} = \sigma_{B1} = 0$; in addition to that $\alpha_B > \beta_{B1} > \beta_{B0}$. Then, B underinvests under either ownership, and B more invests under $A_B = 1$ than$A_B = 0$.

The comparative statics suggest that an increase in levels (importance) of the relation-specific skill for B falls into increases inα_B, β_1, and β_{B1}, enhancing the integration likelihood. An increase in the relation-specific skill for S also increases $\sigma_0$and σ_1, since S can use the skill in dealing with another potential buyer without the bilateral trade with B. These parameter changes, however, are irrelevant to a change in the likelihood of vertical integration.

Regarding specificity, an increase in levels corresponds to decreases in $\sigma_0$and σ_1 for S, with irrelevant effects on the integration. The increased specificity also reduces the parameters β_0, β_1, $\beta_{B0,}$ and β_{B1}. When we interpret the reductions as an increase in the marginal *people* specificity without any changes in the asset specificity, the equal-sized reductions in β_{B0}, and β_{B1} lead to an increase in the integration likelihood. Otherwise, when interpreting the reductions as an increase in the marginal asset specificity without changes in the people specificity, the fall of β_{B0} by more than β_{B1} would also increase the probability of vertical integration.

3.3.2.2 Model 2: B's Investment Creates Relation-Specific Skill for S

As an alternative to Model 1 with the exogenous acquisition of the relation-specific skill for S, suppose that B's investments create the relation-specific skill for S. It is assumed that only B has a non-contractible investment, that $\alpha_B > \sigma_{B0} > \sigma_{B1} > 0$ and that$\alpha_B > \beta_{B1} \geq \beta_{B0} = 0$. The second assumption corresponds to a situation where the benefits for S are largest in a trade with B exclusively making a non-contractible investment. Then, B divests and further invests when owing the asset.

An increase in levels (importance) of the relation-specific skill for B increasesα_B and β_{B1}, resulting in an enhanced integration probability. An increase in the importance of the skill for S also increases σ_{B0} and σ_{B1}, since S can use some of the relation-specific skill in dealing with another buyer. The importance of the skill for S would also increase the likelihood of the vertical integration.

More specificity of the skill for S is depicted by decreases in σ_0, σ_1, σ_{B0} and σ_{B1}, which results in an increase either in the marginal *people* specificity (equal-sized reductions of σ_{B0} and σ_{B1}) or marginal *asset* specificity (a decrease in σ_{B0} at least as much as one inσ_{B1}, due to close ties of the skill to the asset) of i_B for S. These reductions in the parameters would decrease the vertical integration. Further, an increase in the specificity for B arises in reductions of β_0 and β_1, still having no effects on the vertical integration.

3.3.2.3 Model 3: S's Investment Creates Relation-Specific Skill for S

Finally, as the other extreme case, suppose that the seller's investments create the relation-specific skill for S, where it is assumed that only S has a non-contractible investment, that $\alpha_S > \sigma_{S0} > \sigma_{S1}$, and that $\beta_{S1} \geq \beta_{S0} = 0$. The last assumption implies that some of S's relation-specific skill is embodied in the upstream asset. Then, S divests and further invests when owing the asset.

More importance of the relation-specific skill for S increases $\alpha_S, \sigma_{S0},$ and σ_{S1}, the relative magnitudes of those rises matter to the integration likelihood. If $\alpha_S, \sigma_{S0},$ and σ_{S1} have an equal increase, then the increase importance of the skill would not have any effect on the probability. Otherwise if an increase in α_S is at least as large as one in σ_{S0}, in turn at least as large as in σ_{S1}, then the net effect of these three parameters is to decrease the integration. More importance for B increases β_{S1} resulting in a reduction of the integration probability.

As for the specificity, more specificity of the skill for S decreases $\sigma_0, \sigma_1, \sigma_{S0},$ and σ_{S1}. Equal-sized reductions of these values would decrease the integration likelihood. If a decrease in σ_{S0} is at least as large as one in σ_{S1} because of the marginal asset specificity, then the net effect on the integration likelihood would be ambiguous, with a sign of the effect depending upon the parameter values. The larger the decline of σ_{S0} compared with σ_{S1}, the more likely the sign would be positive. More specificity of the skill for B also decreases β_0 and β_1, still being irrelevant to the likelihood.

3.3.2.4 Comparative Statics Results

Table 3.1 summarizes the signs of the effect on the integration likelihood, resulting from the comparative statics analysis. The three specific models address the extreme situations where the relation-specific skill for the seller is created either exogenously by a non-contractible investment of the buyer, or by an investment of the seller itself. The models also provide qualitatively different implications in terms of the effects on the integration likelihood. We match our estimation results with the qualitative implications later on.

Table 3.1 Comparative Statics: "People" means the marginal people specificity for B or S of i_B or i_S. Similarly, "asset" is the marginal asset specificity for B or S of i_B or i_S

Effect on likelihood of integration	More importance of relation-specific skill		More specificity			
	Buyer	Seller	Buyer		Seller	
			People	Asset	People	Asset
Model 1: Exogenous relation-specific skill	(+)	(0)	(+)	(+)	(0)	
Model 2: B's investments create relation-specific skill for S	(+)	(+)	(0)		(−)	(−)
Model 3: S's investments create relation-specific skill for S	(−)	(−)	(0)		(−)	?

3.4 Estimation

3.4.1 Data

We use a combined panel data of the *Basic Survey of Japanese Business Structure and Activities* (Ministry of Economy, Trade and Industry)[2], *Census of Manufactures* (Ministry of Economy, Trade and Industry)[3], and annual magazine *Japanese Automotive Parts Industry* (Japan Auto Parts Industries Association) from 1995 to 2006, compiled from the works of name-based aggregation with a key code of permanent enterprise-numbering in enterprise-name lists provided by the Research Institute of Economy, Trade and Industry (RIETI).

The data set consists of Japanese enterprises from 1995 to 2006, with a sample size 603,505. The *Basic Survey of Japanese Business Structure and Activities* reports for each enterprise the name of, if any, a parent company (the number of the observations 492,241), and the parent company's ownership ratio of a subsidiary. A subsidiary is a company in which a certain company (parent company) owns more than 50% of the voting rights. It includes a company in which the subsidiary, or the parent company and the subsidiary combined, owns more than 50% of the voting rights (deemed subsidiary) and a company is practically controlled by the subsidiary or jointly by the parent company and the subsidiary, even if they own only 50% or lower voting rights. The survey also reports sales value and purchase ratios of a subsidiary with

[2] The survey covers enterprises having 50 or more employees, a paid-up capital or investment fund of over 30 million yen, and operating under the mining, manufacturing, wholesale and retail trade, and eating and drinking places (excluding "other eating and drinking places").

[3] We cover Questionnaire A for establishments with 30 or more employees, Questionnaire B for establishments with 29 or fewer employees, and The Report by Commodity.

the affiliated companies. An affiliated company is one in which a certain company (parent company) directly owns no less than 20% but no more than 50% of the voting rights. It includes any company that may have a significant impact due to owning more than 15% of the voting rights.

By virtue of the data links, we can also identify each enterprise not only by the names of products it produces at the establishments acquired by the *Census of Manufactures*, but also by participation in the associations for technology cooperation founded between auto manufacturers and subcontractors on a first tier, as reported in the annual *Japanese Automotive Parts Industry*. Among the numerous auto parts, we pick up five major components as product items in the *Census of Manufactures*: "parts, attachments and accessories of internal combustion engines for motor vehicles;" "parts of driving, transmission and operating units;" "parts of suspension and brake systems;" "parts of chassis and bodies;" and "parts, attachments and accessories of auxiliary equipment for internal combustion engines." Enterprises have a dummy variable of 1 for establishments with these product items, or 0 otherwise. The *Japanese Automotive Parts Industry* also reports affiliations with the 10 largest associations for technology cooperation: Daihatsu Kyoyu-kai; Hino Kyoryoku-kai; Isuzu Kyowa- kai; Youko-kai (for Mazda Motor Corporation); Nissho-kai (for Nissan); Subaru Yuhi-kai; Suzuki Kyoryoku-kyodo-kumiai; Kyoho-kai (for Toyota); Kyoryoku-kai in 2006 or affiliations in other years for Mitsubishi; and the ones for Honda. Unfortunately, we omit a dummy variable for Suzuki Kyoryoku-kyodo-kumiai due to some discontinuities in the listing. Whether a parent company or the subsidiary joins any association is measured with each set of 9 dummy variables running 0 or 1. We alternate two of the parent's association dummy variables, one where zeroes are assigned for companies without a parent in a year; and the other where the companies concerned are processed as missing values.

We are interested in how rigid the memberships of the supplier associations are, as qualified by the Asanuma hypothesis. The industrial composition of the member suppliers is almost constant over time in our data. Manufacture of transportation equipment accounts for, though gradually declining, half of the members. The second-largest sector is wholesale trade with around 10% share. The other industries with more than 5% share are: manufacture of iron and steel; manufacture of general machinery; and manufacture of electrical machinery, equipment, and supplies. Our data also indicate drastic changes in membership participations. Table 3.2 shows the entry and exit rates of changes of enterprises in each supplier association from 1995 to 2000 or from 2000 to 2006. A few enterprises have entered multiple associations to cooperate in the technology on auto parts. In contrast, some firms exited the associations during 1995–2000, with the exit rates even higher during 2000–2006. The low metabolic rates look indicative of a declining role of supplier associations in the acquisition of the relation-specific skill, invalidating the Asanuma hypothesis.

Table 3.2 Entry and exit rates of changes in enterprises of supplier associations

Supplier Associations % Changes	Entry		Exit	
	From 1995 to 2000	From 2000 to 2006	From 1995 to 2000	From 2000 to 2006
Daihatsu	0.05	0.04	5.63	12.35
Hino	0.04	0.12	5.88	14.86
Honda	0.11	0.24	4.32	24.68
Isuzu	0.06	0.12	12.11	20.86
Mazda	0.02	0.02	5.85	18.45
Mitsubishi	0.03	0.02	3.68	60.07
Nissan	0.02	0.05	15.03	18.71
Subaru	0.02	0.04	9.21	19.05
Toyota	0.06	0.03	5.2	13.37

3.4.2 Method and Result

We estimate a single equation of the likelihood of vertical integration with regressors of proxy variables for the importance of the relation-specific skill and degree of specificity. Our methodology considers both censored data on a dependent variable and endogenous regressors in the estimated single equation.

3.4.2.1 Censored Data

The dependent variable in the estimated equation is a parent company's ownership ratio of a subsidiary. Without any parent's name in the questionnaire for an enterprise, the producer should be assigned a value of zero. The dependent variable has data censoring and is thus required to apply censored regression models, among which we choose a Tobit model as follows:

$$y_{it} = \mathbf{max}\left(0, y_{it}^{*}\right) \tag{3.4}$$

$$y_{it}^{*} = x_{it}\gamma + z_{it}\delta + u_{it}$$

where an error term u_{it} follows normal distribution $\mathrm{N}\left(0, \sigma^2\right)$ conditional upon realized values x_{it} and z_{it}. The general setup of the PRT suggests that the parent's ownership ratio y_{it} of a subsidiary i at a year t has two determinants: the importance x_{it} of the relation-specific skill for a subsidiary or a parent, and the degree of the specificity z_{it} for each of them.

The proxy variables for the importance x_{it} of the relation-specific skill are the 10 dummy variables for participation of either a subsidiary or a parent in each association. The proxies for the specificity z_{it} of the skill for a subsidiary or a parent are the sales value or purchase ratios of a subsidiary with the affiliated companies, respectively. Moreover, we add to the estimated equation some control variables, year-dummy variables for 1995–2005, and industry-dummy variables. We pick the 24 industries listed by enterprises belonging to any supplier association, according to 2-digit codes in the *Japan Standard Industrial Classification*[4]. We present first estimation results in case of the parent's association dummy variables, with zeroes assigned for no-parent companies. Later for robustness, we show the results using the other measurement of the parent association dummy variables.

The estimates of the Tobit models are shown in Table 3.3. We alternate a set of the independent variables chosen for the importance and specificity proxies. It is evident, on the one hand, that both the specificity variables (sale value and parent's purchase ratios) are significant with positive signs. It suggests that model 1 of the exogenous relation-specific skill might be plausible enough to render the Japanese auto parts industry. On the other hand, almost all coefficients on the dummy variables for the subsidiary's participation in any of the associations are significantly negative, while a few coefficients on the parent's dummy variable for the participation are significantly negative for Toyota and Mitsubishi, or significantly positive for Nissan and Mazda. The patterns imply that for Toyota and Mitsubishi, it is likely that model 3 is valid, where a seller's non-contractible investment creates the relation-specific skill for itself. Further, for Nissan and Mazda, if anything, model 1 of the exogenous skill acquisition would be applicable.

3.4.2.2 Endogenous Regressors

In the Tobit regression models above, the proxy variables x_{it} and z_{it} for the importance and specificity on the right-hand side should be likely treated as endogenous. In the general setup of the PRT, investment decisions i_B and i_S made by a buyer and seller are contingent on asset ownership $A_B = 0 or 1$. The importance of B's and S's investments in improving the upstream asset affects the likelihood of vertical integration, which in turn has a bearing on the investments themselves. Additionally, for the degree of

[4] Among 26 relevant industry dummy variables containing collinearities detected among instruments in the estimation below, we use 24 industry dummy variables for general construction work, including public and private construction work; manufacture of food; manufacture of textile mill products; manufacture of lumber and wood products, except furniture; manufacture of furniture and fixtures; manufacture of pulp, paper, and paper products; printing and allied industries; manufacture of chemical and allied products; manufacture of petroleum and coal products; manufacture of plastic products; manufacture of rubber products; manufacture of ceramic, stone and clay products; manufacture of iron and steel; manufacture of non-ferrous metals and products; manufacture of fabricated metal products; manufacture of general machinery; manufacture of electrical machinery, equipment and supplies; manufacture of transportation equipment; manufacture of precision instruments and machinery; miscellaneous manufacturing industries; transport; wholesale trade; retail trade; and services, n.e.c.

Table 3.3 Tobit regression: the parent's association dummy variables with zeroes assigned for companies without parent in a year; asterisk symbols *, **, and *** mean significance level 10%, 5%, and 1%

Ownership ratio	(1)# of obs. = 18,665		(2)# 18,665		(3)# 85,803		(4)# 28,504		(5)# 31,735	
	Coef	t-value	Coef	t-value	Coef	t-value	Coef	t-value	Coef	t-value
Sale value ratio	0.142***	20.18	0.159***	22.31			0.137***	27.02		
Purchase ratio	0.085***	13.27	0.084***	12.98					0.069***	14.74
Subsidiary										
toyota	−11.50**	−2.44			−10.45***	−6.21	−4.05	−1.16		
Nissan	−23.84***	−5.57			−23.18***	−12.46	−16.13***	−4.75		
Mitsubishi	−13.71***	−3.52			−10.37***	−6.13	−16.80***	−5.41		
Mazda	−4.39	−1.12			−12.89***	−7.58	−2.93	−0.96		
Isuzu	−10.03**	−2.49			−11.12***	−6.54	−2.46	−0.83		
Daihatsu	−5.89	−1.30			−11.38***	−5.88	−19.99***	−5.85		
Hino	−14.03***	−3.50			−12.64***	−7.04	−16.91***	−5.51		
Honda	−14.30***	−4.60			−26.16***	−20.26	−15.97***	−6.82		
Subaru	−6.63	−1.47			−6.25***	−3.21	−17.12***	−4.98		
Parent										
Toyota	−1.93*	−1.76			−1.83***	−3.55			−1.99***	−2.70
Nissan	6.03***	4.92			3.74***	7.15			5.21***	6.30
Mitsubishi	−4.81***	−4.34			−2.29***	−4.07			−2.70***	−3.55
Mazda	4.59***	3.33			3.71***	5.96			4.18***	4.36

(continued)

Table 3.3 (continued)

Ownership ratio	(1)# of obs. = 18,665		(2)# 18,665		(3)# 85,803		(4)# 28,504		(5)# 31,735	
	Coef	t-value	Coef	t-value	Coef	t-value	Coef	t-value	Coef	t-value
Isuzu	2.18	1.47			1.82***	2.89			0.166	0.16
Daihatsu	−0.384	−0.28			1.10*	1.76			−0.037	−0.04
Hino	2.20*	1.69			1.76***	2.84			0.655	0.73
Honda	1.86*	1.67			3.45***	7.55			2.04***	2.63
Subaru	−1.72	−1.22			−1.48**	−2.55			−1.57	−1.61

specificity, the proxy variables cannot break down a change in the specificity a buyer or seller incurs in the exogenous parametersα_B, β_{B0}, and β_{B1}, or α_S, σ_{S0}, and σ_{S1}, indicating marginal people and asset specificity. Changes in the parameters affect the integration likelihood and specificity proxy measures simultaneously. For these reasons, it is possible for us to consider the endogeneity of regressors in the binary regression models.

One estimation is the Tobit model with endogenous regressors of only continuous variables instrumented with some instruments. Otherwise, if we include binary, discrete, or censored variables as endogenous regressors in the estimation, the estimator will generate inconsistent estimates (Angrist, 2001). The other method is the special regressor estimator of Lewbel et al. (2012), where to address the problems of endogenous regressors of binary variables, a linear two-stage least-square estimator can be applied to a probit model. A special regressor is chosen among the continuously distributed, possibly exogenous, regressors with a large support.

IV Tobit Models First, in the Tobit models, we allow some of the variables.

z_{it} to be endogenous.

$$y_{it} = \mathbf{max}(0, \boldsymbol{x_{it}\gamma} + z_{it}\boldsymbol{\delta} + \boldsymbol{u_{it}}) \tag{3.5}$$

$$z_{it} = w_{it}\theta + \omega_{it}$$

where (u_{it}, ω_{it}) are zero-mean normally distributed, and instruments ω_{it} are incorporated for identification. The IV Tobit model, however, can address as endogenous regressors in the Tobit model continuous variables such as a proxy for the specificityz_{it}, and not binary variables like a proxyx_{it}, for the importance of the skill. We estimate the IV Tobit model with the endogenous variables z_{it} and instrumentsw_{it}. The instruments are the five product dummy variables, and a logarithm of capitals, besides the independent variables.

The estimates of the IV Tobit models using the two-step estimator (Newey, 1987) are indicated in Table 3.4. After the IV regressions, coefficients only on the subsidiary's specificity proxy variables remain significantly positive in all the cases. It suggests that model 1 is close to what happens in the auto parts industry in Japan. As for the effect of the importance, there seems to be weaker evidence supporting model 3, relative to the original Tobit regressions. A few exceptions to apply to model 3 are Daihatsu, Hino, and Mitsubishi. Similar results are seen in Tables 3.5 and 3.6 when we use the other measurement of the parent's association dummy variable, with missing values assigned for the companies without a parent.

Special Regressor Probit Models Second, for the special regressor probit model, we consider a binary choice dependent variable d_{it}, which takes a value 1 if the parent's ownership ratio y_{it} of a subsidiary i at a year t is larger than or equal to 50%, or a value 0 otherwise. The special regressor estimation of a probit model (Lewbel et al., 2012) assumes an exogenous regressor v_{it}, continuously distributed with a large support.

Table 3.4 IV Tobit regression: the parent's association dummy variables with zeroes assigned for companies without parent in a year; asterisk symbols *, **, and *** mean significance level 10%, 5%, and 1%

Ownership ratio	(1)# of obs. = 18,575		(2)# 18,575		(3)# 28,327		(4)# 21,789	
	Coef	z-value	Coef	z-value	Coef	z-value	Coef	z-value
Sale value ratio	3.52***	13.42	2.62***	25.02	2.31***	29.79		
Purchase ratio	−0.871	−1.25	0.157	1.24			5.05***	8.35
Subsidiary								
Toyota	17.87	1.01			−4.59	−0.50		
Nissan	34.46**	2.16			17.60**	2.00		
Mitsubishi	1.15	0.08			−0.268	−0.03		
Mazda	12.72	0.89			4.36	0.55		
Isuzu	3.67	0.21			14.64*	1.87		
Daihatsu	−18.52	−1.13			−17.61**	−1.99		
Hino	−45.40***	−2.95			−31.58***	−3.92		
Honda	20.94*	1.76			9.94	1.59		
Subaru	5.92	0.36			−11.74	−1.35		
Parent								
Toyota	−18.88**	−4.41					−13.61**	−2.23
Nissan	−6.93	−1.40					18.01***	2.62
Mitsubishi	4.41	0.64					−38.11***	−5.22
Mazda	−6.95	−1.03					25.54***	3.21
Isuzu	10.25*	1.81					−1.80	−0.22
Daihatsu	18.00*	1.95					−47.79**	−5.05
Hino	12.06*	1.74					−34.95***	−4.20
Honda	−12.59*	−1.78					40.87***	5.30
Subaru	−2.71	−0.50					0.914	0.12

$$\boldsymbol{d_{it}} = \mathbf{I}(\boldsymbol{v_{it}} + \boldsymbol{x_{it}\gamma} + \boldsymbol{z_{it}\delta} + \boldsymbol{u_{it}} \geq 0) \tag{3.6}$$

$$v_{it} = \omega_{it}\eta + \varepsilon_{it}$$

where an indicator function I(•) takes a value 1 if its argument • is true, and a value 0 otherwise. The special regressor estimator is obtained by first constructing $\mathrm{T} = \frac{d_{it} - I(v_{it} \geq 0)}{f(v_{it}|\omega_{it}, x_{it}, z_{it})}$, where the special regressor v_{it} is demeaned and a one-dimensional kernel density estimator is used for the conditional density $f(v_{it}|\omega_{it}, x_{it}, z_{it}) = f(v_{it}|\omega_{it}) = f(\varepsilon_{it})$ of a residual estimate ε_{it}, and second applying a two-stage least square regression to $\mathrm{T} = x_{it}\gamma + z_{it}\delta + \tilde{u}_{it}$ with instruments ω_{it}. The estimation

Table 3.5 Tobit regression: the parent's association dummy variables with missing values assigned for companies without parent in a year; asterisk symbols *,**, and *** mean significance level 10, 5, and 1%

Tobit	(1)# of obs. = 4768		(2)# 20,896		(3)# 9181	
	Coef	t-value	Coef	t-value	Coef	t-value
Sale value ratio	0.097***	9.98				
Purchase ratio	0.027***	2.88			0.031***	4.02
Subsidiary						
Toyota	−11.23***	−2.79	−12.41***	−8.29		
Nissan	−27.89***	−8.27	−23.71***	−14.89		
Mitsubishi	−20.55***	−6.37	−13.40***	−8.94		
Mazda	−10.29***	−2.99	−11.84***	−7.98		
Isuzu	−4.67	−1.25	−11.53***	−7.36		
Daihatsu	−1.67	−0.38	−9.43***	−5.16		
Hino	−9.59***	−2.65	−10.00***	−6.02		
Honda	−25.24***	−9.08	−33.80***	−29.67		
Subaru	−5.22	−1.41	−6.88***	−4.13		
Parent						
Toyota	−2.64***	−3.09	−1.82***	−4.52	−2.42***	−3.54
Nissan	3.34***	3.60	1.31***	3.23	2.73***	3.67
Mitsubishi	−3.47***	−4.27	−1.50***	−3.51	−2.16***	−3.26
Mazda	1.13	1.10	1.68***	3.48	2.14***	2.53
Isuzu	2.09*	1.93	2.32***	4.82	1.32	1.47
Daihatsu	0.244	0.24	0.509	1.07	−0.146	−0.18
Hino	1.74*	1.83	0.926*	1.96	0.510	0.65
Honda	1.47*	1.66	1.87***	4.88	1.03	1.42
Subaru	−1.44	−1.41	−1.28***	−2.93	−1.17	−1.39

can be carried out even when including the endogenous binary-choice regressors x_{it} proxying the importance of the relation-specific skills.

However, since we have the 18 endogenous binary-choice regressors x_{it} measured with the participation of either a subsidiary or a parent into nine associations, we cannot practically find at least an equal number of relevant instruments. So we have to count only a partial set of the 18 regressors as the endogenous variables, especially a pair of the dummy variables for a subsidiary and a parent's participation in each association. Accordingly, the number of endogenous regressors is four, including two continuous variables proxying the specificity z_{it}.

Regarding the special regressorv_{it}, which is required to be an exogenous continuously-distributed variable with a large support, we specify either of the two

Table 3.6 IV Tobit regression: the parent's association dummy variables with missing values assigned for companies without parent in a year; asterisk symbols *, **, and *** mean significance level 10%, 5%, and 1%

IV Tobit	(1)# of obs. = 4745		(2)# 4745		(3)# 8288		(4)# 5336	
	Coef	z–value	Coef	z–value	Coef	z–value	Coef	z–value
Sale value ratio	1.49***	6.21	1.60***	14.46	1.09***	12.47		
Purchase ratio	−0.545	−1.10	−0.030	−0.38			1.21***	5.06
Subsidiary								
Toyota	−1.34	−0.13			−5.21	−0.95		
Nissan	2.63	0.27			−1.79	−0.35		
Mitsubishi	−18.64*	−1.77			−9.30*	−1.92		
Mazda	−2.76	−0.30			−6.92	−1.44		
Isuzu	4.96	0.46			11.94**	2.38		
Daihatsu	−6.74	−0.64			−20.29***	−3.53		
Hino	−20.67**	−2.32			−23.19***	−4.51		
Honda	−12.72*	−1.69			−11.13***	−2.78		
Subaru	4.11	0.47			−16.50***	−3.29		
Parent								
Toyota	−10.70***	−3.74					−1.67	−1.01
Nissan	−1.98	−0.66					7.50***	3.65
Mitsubishi	0.942	0.20					−12.46***	−5.23
Mazda	−0.756	−0.19					6.45***	2.76
Isuzu	4.19	1.44					2.09	0.99
Daihatsu	8.44	1.42					−10.63***	−3.51
Hino	6.31	1.34					-10.16***	-3.57
Honda	-5.44	-1.22					10.86***	4.03
Subaru	-3.15	-1.18					-1.29	-0.64

firm attributes: current asset ratio to total assets; and firm age (both from the *Basic Survey of Japanese Business Structure and Activities*).

Tables 3.7, 3.8, 3.9, 3.10, 3.11, 3.12, 3.13, 3.14 and 3.15 indicate the regression results. As measured with the coefficients on the sale value ratio in the estimations, the effects of the subsidiary's specificity are still evident. Among the evidence, there are significantly negative effects in the cases where the current asset ratio is used as the special regressor when missing values are applied to companies without a parent. It suggests validity of model 3's comparative statics. Concerning the effects of the importance of the subsidiary or parent's participation in the association, more meager results are shown, except for a few cases suggestive of model 3 where the subsidiary's self-investment creates the relation-specific skill.

Table 3.7 Special regressor probit regression (3.1) Endogenous Toyota dummy variables

Probit special regressor	Missing values for companies without parent				Zeroes for companies without parent			
	Current asset ratio: # of obs. = 4529		Firm age: #4514		Current asset ratio: # of obs. = 17,731		Firm age: #17,674	
	Coef	z-value	Coef	z-value	Coef	z-value	Coef	z-value
Endogenous variables								
Sale value ratio	−0.93	−2.48**	0.60	1.45	0.60	5.09***	2.14	10.8***
Purchase ratio	0.08	0.09	0.36	0.38	−0.28	−0.92	−0.69	−1.28
Toyota subsidiary	200.05	2.22**	−33.01	−0.17	96.76	1.04	189.53	1.04
Toyota parent	−100.69	−0.84	121.27	1.24	−24.30	−0.26	−192.51	−1.16
Exogenous variables								
Subsidiary nissan	−63.90	−2.74***	24.40	1.06	−5.19	−0.22	−14.92	−0.37
Mitsubishi	−11.75	−0.66	−4.53	−0.37	−4.72	−0.7	4.57	0.41
Mazda	−13.97	−1.04	12.80	0.61	−0.90	−0.08	−13.12	−0.5
Isuzu	−22.64	−0.78	−23.51	−0.6	−11.54	−1.05	−9.59	−0.49
Daihatsu	−91.60	−1.59	−15.93	−0.16	−42.33	−1.18	−48.45	−0.79
Hino	−23.54	−1.5	−14.01	−0.5	−24.83	−1.53	−56.74	−1.86*
Honda	−50.93	−3.93***	−4.98	−0.24	−12.39	−1.13	−11.18	−0.52
Subaru	−16.51	−1.34	3.98	0.3	−2.67	−0.3	−9.11	−0.57
Parent Nissan	33.73	1.03	−32.50	−1.28	1.65	0.05	57.39	0.99
Mitsubishi	−4.08	−0.72	1.67	0.22	0.73	0.17	−2.63	−0.34
Mazda	9.40	0.79	−11.06	−0.88	4.88	0.32	28.57	0.96
Isuzu	8.39	1.72*	−4.70	−1.27	6.97	1.27	8.25	1.2
Daihatsu	40.78	0.96	−40.75	−1.22	19.56	0.7	61.08	1.31
Hino	17.99	0.66	−28.07	−1.27	7.61	0.42	40.64	1.22
Honda	5.53	0.77	−0.10	−0.01	0.93	0.12	8.99	0.54
Subaru	−11.09	−1.2	8.49	1.33	−4.96	−0.53	−15.30	−1.05

Table 3.8 Special regressor probit regression (3.2) Endogenous Nissan dummy

Probit special regressor	Missing values for companies without parent				Zeroes for companies without parent			
	Current asset ratio: # of obs. = 4529		Firm age: #4514		Current asset ratio: # of obs. = 17,731		Firm age: #17,674	
	Coef	z-value	Coef	z-value	Coef	z-value	Coef	z-value
Endogenous variables								
Sale value ratio	−0.90	−1.7*	−0.59	−0.65	0.60	4.2***	2.00	8.63***
Purchase ratio	−0.05	−0.08	0.66	0.74	−0.28	−0.84	−0.48	−0.97
Nissan subsidiary	2.08	0.01	−419.85	−1.65	31.86	0.35	−48.40	−0.29
Nissan parent	−37.41	−0.48	172.15	1.43	0.41	0.01	103.40	1.05
Exogenous variables								
Subsidiary toyota	−24.55	−1.43	44.94	1.45	1.59	0.11	34.00	1.52
Mitsubishi	−21.56	−1.26	15.15	0.74	−6.90	−0.63	10.25	0.65
Mazda	4.25	0.29	3.05	0.17	1.50	0.17	12.18	0.92
Isuzu	−23.34	−0.65	96.60	1.53	−7.85	−0.44	17.38	0.54
Daihatsu	5.23	0.41	−35.33	−1.34	−1.23	−0.14	−12.80	−0.83
Hino	5.44	0.43	11.02	0.47	−12.20	−1.39	−31.40	−2.36**
Honda	−28.03	−3.2***	−14.04	−1.2	−3.56	−0.66	5.26	0.62
Subaru	−14.90	−0.31	132.06	1.59	−7.79	−0.23	33.97	0.47
Parent Toyota	9.15	0.5	−34.90	−1.49	−9.79	−0.56	−42.32	−1.58
Mitsubishi	5.91	0.45	−30.12	−1.38	0.71	0.08	−13.38	−0.8
Mazda	−7.72	−0.94	17.29	1.45	−7.71	−2.03**	0.76	0.13
Isuzu	18.89	0.82	−61.55	−1.51	5.23	0.28	−35.82	−1.03
Daihatsu	5.50	0.56	14.64	1.07	16.27	1.71*	27.55	1.81*
Hino	2.41	0.39	−5.93	−0.81	4.87	1.29	2.83	0.53
Honda	6.13	1.47	−0.82	−0.13	−1.12	−0.22	−16.20	−1.97**
Subaru	7.42	0.39	−36.96	−1.3	−5.14	−0.33	−29.93	−1.12

Table 3.9 Special regressor probit regression (3.3) Endogenous Mitsubishi dummy variables

Probit special regressor	Missing values for companies without parent				Zeroes for companies without parent			
	Current Asset Ratio: # of obs. = 4529		Firm Age: #4514		Current Asset Ratio: # of obs. = 17,731		Firm Age: #17,674	
	Coef	z-value	Coef	z-value	Coef	z-value	Coef	z-value
Endogenous variables								
Sale value ratio	−0.96	−2.2**	0.93	2.38**	0.52	3.53***	2.17	5.25***
Purchase ratio	0.99	0.94	−0.99	−0.99	0.09	0.15	−1.17	−0.6
Mitsubishi subsidiary	−154.94	−0.74	33.53	0.2	−298.78	−0.87	194.44	0.2
Mitsubishi parent	181.76	1.33	−138.20	−0.97	129.78	0.75	−193.92	−0.36
Exogenous variables								
Subsidiary toyota	−27.11	−1.27	15.31	0.83	3.64	0.39	16.70	0.87
Nissan	−9.78	−0.29	−7.97	−0.27	45.68	0.84	−11.85	−0.08
Mazda	6.09	0.2	1.54	0.05	50.17	0.94	−13.02	−0.08
Isuzu	−14.93	−0.59	−1.97	−0.09	26.89	0.75	−16.75	−0.19
Daihatsu	66.54	0.89	−33.01	−0.55	61.66	0.81	−55.49	−0.28
Hino	55.23	0.88	−45.37	−0.86	56.03	0.73	−79.73	−0.36
Honda	−15.39	−0.64	−9.70	−0.54	25.14	0.76	−7.93	−0.09
Subaru	−6.85	−0.38	10.96	0.64	15.13	0.88	9.44	0.28
Parent Toyota	8.48	1.06	−13.66	−1.39	−3.78	−0.6	−19.87	−1.03
Nissan	−24.59	−1.13	22.45	0.92	−24.89	−0.91	29.59	0.32
Mazda	−29.72	−1.44	22.40	1.08	−23.82	−1.05	22.84	0.36
Isuzu	−14.20	−0.82	15.67	0.78	−9.69	−0.44	33.04	0.39
Daihatsu	−48.43	−1.08	50.07	0.99	−22.37	−0.45	73.20	0.42
Hino	−45.31	−1.3	33.76	0.97	−26.18	−0.62	48.00	0.42
Honda	3.17	0.43	−5.24	−0.82	−7.86	−0.74	−0.90	−0.06
Subaru	6.93	0.82	−9.32	−0.87	2.94	0.31	−14.04	−0.42

Table 3.10 Special regressor probit regression (3.4) Endogenous Mazda dummy variables

Probit special regressor	Missing values for companies without parent				Zeroes for companies without parent			
	Current asset ratio: # of obs. = 4529		Firm age: #4514		Current asset ratio: # of obs. = 17,731		Firm age: #17,674	
	Coef	z–value	Coef	z–value	Coef	z–value	Coef	z–value
Endogenous variables								
Sale value ratio	0.76	0.36	0.51	0.49	0.51	4.13***	3.75	0.67
Purchase ratio	−2.89	−0.66	2.92	0.6	−0.16	−0.39	−8.41	−0.33
Mazda subsidiary	1105.37	0.81	−523.41	−0.63	−123.45	−1.04	−1051.56	−0.35
Mazda parent	−148.32	−0.47	378.95	0.65	27.20	0.38	−1246.46	−0.3
Exogenous variables								
Subsidiary toyota	−79.04	−0.86	46.46	0.64	12.00	1.12	63.08	0.46
Nissan	−114.27	−1.25	13.55	0.36	11.38	0.7	256.98	0.37
Mitsubishi	−220.74	−0.86	86.04	0.56	16.33	0.71	312.94	0.34
Isuzu	−190.37	−0.84	110.00	0.6	18.14	0.89	172.53	0.36
Daihatsu	−187.60	−0.79	84.71	0.62	12.30	0.76	134.68	0.33
Hino	−139.06	−0.8	26.54	0.31	4.64	0.33	36.73	0.2
Honda	−47.54	−1.29	13.50	0.34	-2.73	-0.53	25.70	0.39
Subaru	−88.72	−0.73	97.11	0.61	20.80	1.51	−62.45	−0.21
Parent Toyota	4.03	0.18	−33.36	−0.73	−12.03	−1.58	112.65	0.27
Nissan	−17.55	−0.53	31.76	0.64	−3.67	−1.33	−46.28	−0.34
Mitsubishi	32.24	0.54	−62.02	−0.65	−2.95	−0.3	176.45	0.31
Isuzu	43.95	0.49	−115.50	−0.67	−4.09	−0.18	402.46	0.3
Daihatsu	37.96	1.04	−12.39	−0.47	16.07	3.97***	7.94	0.22
Hino	38.83	0.6	−63.97	−0.66	0.74	0.07	198.61	0.31
Honda	−3.56	−0.21	−7.99	−0.48	−2.30	−0.51	23.78	0.21
Subaru	38.57	0.38	−130.73	−0.64	−16.36	−0.6	458.89	0.3

Table 3.11 Special regressor probit regression (3.5) Endogenous Isuzu dummy variables

Probit special regressor	Missing values for companies without parent				Zeroes for companies without parent			
	Current Asset Ratio: # of obs. = 4529		Firm Age: #4514		Current Asset Ratio: # of obs. = 17,731		Firm Age: #17,674	
	Coef	z–value	Coef	z–value	Coef	z–value	Coef	z–value
Endogenous variables								
Sale value ratio	−0.72	−1.53	0.45	1.31	0.56	2.88***	2.23	8.01***
Purchase ratio	−0.18	−0.27	0.08	0.16	−0.27	−0.57	−0.96	−1.37
Isuzu subsidiary	−29.48	−0.25	−190.48	−2.01**	−104.68	−0.84	45.46	0.15
Isuzu parent	−92.39	−0.62	136.89	1.67*	30.50	0.19	−131.39	−0.72
Exogenous variables								
Subsidiary toyota	8.79	0.35	1.72	0.09	11.60	0.54	30.33	0.91
Nissan	−31.49	−1.79*	34.76	2**	16.95	0.87	20.16	0.39
Mitsubishi	−21.66	−0.93	14.24	0.96	9.36	0.44	−6.00	−0.16
Mazda	2.45	0.09	36.88	1.59	21.44	0.82	0.31	0.01
Daihatsu	−1.92	−0.15	3.46	0.32	−0.12	−0.01	−11.43	−0.74
Hino	7.74	0.32	10.01	0.56	5.75	0.3	−37.02	−0.86
Honda	−28.39	−1.51	16.71	1.14	7.66	0.46	−1.34	−0.04
Subaru	−7.63	−0.26	23.98	1.39	17.71	0.62	−16.07	−0.35
Parent toyota	0.36	0.12	−3.24	−1.12	−8.56	−1.77*	−10.64	−2.57**
Nissan	24.21	0.76	−34.59	−1.74*	−10.39	−0.29	26.78	0.61
Mitsubishi	8.67	0.63	−12.86	−1.45	−0.36	−0.03	17.45	0.91
Mazda	22.10	0.55	−37.91	−1.58	−14.30	−0.33	34.47	0.67
Daihatsu	7.16	0.91	6.30	0.93	16.45	2.29**	5.85	0.58
Hino	19.73	0.7	−23.54	−1.68*	1.22	0.04	27.63	0.89
Honda	18.66	0.89	−21.36	−1.83*	−4.10	−0.18	10.54	0.41
Subaru	16.35	0.56	−24.06	−1.59	−8.43	−0.27	23.98	0.72

Table 3.12 Special regressor probit regression (3.6) Endogenous Daihatsu dummy variables

Probit special regressor	Missing values for companies without parent				Zeroes for companies without parent			
	Current Asset Ratio: # of obs. = 4529		Firm Age: #4514		Current Asset Ratio: # of obs. = 17,731		Firm Age: #17,674	
	Coef	z–value	Coef	z–value	Coef	z–value	Coef	z–value
Endogenous variables								
Sale value ratio	−1.07	−2.41**	0.88	1.83*	0.32	1	1.93	7.53***
Purchase ratio	1.01	0.44	−1.09	−0.43	0.73	0.64	0.01	0.02
Daihatsu subsidiary	−446.04	−1.59	29.36	0.11	−90.42	−0.7	41.30	0.31
Daihatsu parent	224.19	0.59	−154.90	−0.38	279.41	1.22	174.89	0.95
Exogenous variables								
Subsidiary toyota	163.09	1.39	17.51	0.18	5.60	0.08	−31.96	−0.47
Nissan	−71.72	−1.98**	19.51	0.47	−19.47	−1.06	19.97	1.06
Mitsubishi	83.62	0.84	−41.46	−0.4	33.38	1.12	20.03	0.71
Mazda	26.59	0.61	8.98	0.24	−0.79	−0.04	2.42	0.15
Isuzu	−34.13	−0.72	14.75	0.26	−22.20	−0.96	−17.13	−0.88
Hino	94.02	1.03	−54.56	−0.51	33.81	0.96	−13.59	−0.46
Honda	−25.16	−1.35	−13.51	−0.79	0.54	0.07	10.12	1.17
Subaru	19.70	0.33	−29.30	−0.45	37.16	1.08	25.24	0.82
Parent Toyota	−47.53	−0.54	28.08	0.33	−61.40	−1.31	−43.20	−1.27
Nissan	37.25	0.59	−24.89	−0.39	38.07	1	19.53	0.7
Mitsubishi	−47.56	−0.55	37.71	0.38	−51.15	−1.09	−31.34	−0.78
Mazda	12.45	0.32	−13.98	−0.32	16.48	0.71	13.25	0.71
Isuzu	24.44	0.67	−16.97	−0.46	29.03	1.45	17.96	1.06
Hino	−105.14	−0.53	79.28	0.37	−130.85	−1.09	−79.34	−0.84
Honda	−22.21	−0.4	18.56	0.34	−29.93	−1.16	−26.96	−1.27
Subaru	−42.33	−0.6	30.80	0.4	−53.80	−1.22	−31.89	−0.89

Table 3.13 Special regressor probit regression (7) Endogenous Hino dummy variables

Probit special regressor	Missing values for companies without parent				Zeroes for companies without parent			
	Current Asset Ratio: # of obs. = 4529		Firm Age: #4514		Current Asset Ratio: # of obs. = 17,731		Firm Age: #17,674	
	Coef	z-value	Coef	z-value	Coef	z-value	Coef	z-value
Endogenous variables								
Sale value ratio	−0.72	−0.54	0.39	0.31	0.68	3.06***	2.18	5.86***
Purchase ratio	−0.84	−0.23	0.36	0.19	−0.65	−0.88	−1.18	−0.92
Hino subsidiary	−540.98	−0.35	445.49	0.49	−49.09	−0.15	−506.97	−0.83
Hino parent	560.74	0.35	−444.25	−0.49	132.75	0.34	637.39	0.7
Exogenous variables								
Subsidiary toyota	49.67	0.26	−67.78	−0.48	5.99	0.1	103.86	0.9
Nissan	0.79	0.01	−33.86	−0.37	5.90	0.19	78.35	1.13
Mitsubishi	65.56	0.28	−71.31	−0.57	−1.37	−0.03	56.19	0.81
Mazda	55.61	0.37	−41.05	−0.56	6.17	0.23	36.33	1
Isuzu	124.30	0.32	−114.56	−0.53	8.73	0.15	85.35	0.74
Daihatsu	169.51	0.36	−135.93	−0.5	11.88	0.18	104.93	0.69
Honda	11.27	0.1	−54.19	−0.57	0.67	0.03	38.49	0.9
Subaru	−130.38	−0.35	99.45	0.47	−18.61	−0.25	−125.51	−0.71
Parent Toyota	−82.01	−0.36	63.81	0.46	−24.92	−0.48	−100.86	−0.8
Nissan	3.69	0.29	−4.26	−0.39	−7.53	−1.07	−10.24	−1.03
Mitsubishi	−76.41	−0.36	60.74	0.5	−16.31	−0.27	−86.58	−0.68
Mazda	−74.17	−0.37	60.48	0.51	−24.80	−0.51	−82.24	−0.72

(continued)

Table 3.13 (continued)

Probit special regressor	Missing values for companies without parent				Zeroes for companies without parent			
	Current Asset Ratio: # of obs. = 4529		Firm Age: #4514		Current Asset Ratio: # of obs. = 17,731		Firm Age: #17,674	
	Coef	z-value	Coef	z-value	Coef	z-value	Coef	z-value
Isuzu	−110.97	−0.33	81.80	0.47	−18.77	−0.24	−121.38	−0.68
Daihatsu	−255.47	−0.34	212.25	0.49	−44.88	−0.23	−306.65	−0.68
Honda	79.54	0.38	−57.20	−0.52	11.94	0.28	60.16	0.62
Subaru	103.94	0.34	−83.41	−0.48	21.66	0.28	124.73	0.7

Table 3.14 Special regressor probit regression (8) Endogenous Honda dummy variables

Probit Special Regressor	Missing values for companies without parent				Zeroes for companies without parent			
	Current Asset Ratio: # of obs. = 4529		Firm Age: #4514		Current Asset Ratio: # of obs. = 17,731		Firm Age: #17,674	
	Coef	z-value	Coef	z-value	Coef	z-value	Coef	z-value
Endogenous variables								
Sale value ratio	−1.27	−0.74	−0.09	−0.16	0.49	3.22***	1.87	7.2***
Purchase ratio	−0.62	−0.51	0.29	0.59	−0.23	−0.72	−0.44	−0.9
Honda subsidiary	−48.00	−0.13	−210.13	−1.93*	−119.20	−0.89	−194.12	−0.96
Honda parent	−131.59	−1.19	98.53	2.1**	75.66	1.27	164.33	1.95*
Exogenous variables								
Subsidiary toyota	−16.44	−0.25	35.58	1.65	29.27	0.92	59.90	1.3
Nissan	−46.46	−1.23	−3.13	−0.26	5.41	0.65	41.31	2.65***
Mitsubishi	−23.24	−0.51	8.19	0.64	10.79	0.53	23.43	0.95
Mazda	3.07	0.22	−4.14	−0.46	7.99	1.17	18.11	1.73*
Isuzu	−2.96	−0.04	43.27	1.64	17.74	0.75	40.05	1.1
Daihatsu	25.60	1.16	−9.39	−0.84	−4.93	−0.43	−11.65	−0.89
Hino	11.36	0.29	0.54	0.03	−3.73	−0.32	−23.51	−1.49
Subaru	−17.11	−0.2	45.27	1.88*	33.83	1.18	60.06	1.2
Parent Toyota	−1.38	−0.21	−0.86	−0.25	−14.06	−2.85***	−27.69	−3.53***
Nissan	10.60	1.08	−0.76	−0.2	−11.72	−1.67*	−20.73	−2.4**
Mitsubishi	10.75	0.89	−5.16	−1.09	−5.14	−0.85	−7.34	−1.04
Mazda	5.96	0.64	−5.28	−0.99	−15.34	−2.09**	−19.47	−2.12**
Isuzu	35.15	1.47	−27.37	−2.51**	−14.40	−0.88	−45.52	−1.91*
Daihatsu	46.87	1.47	−24.23	−1.88*	0.54	0.04	−24.79	−1.31
Hino	−16.29	−1.12	8.38	1.13	15.42	1.59	27.90	2.25**
Subaru	34.61	1.07	−27.15	−1.98**	−27.53	−1.53	−54.67	−2.05**

Table 3.15 Special regressor probit regression (9) Endogenous Subaru dummy variables

Probit Special Regressor	Missing values for companies without parent				Zeroes for companies without parent			
	Current Asset Ratio: # of obs. = 4529		Firm Age: #4514		Current Asset Ratio: # of obs. = 17,731		Firm Age: #17,674	
	Coef	z-value	Coef	z-value	Coef	z-value	Coef	z-value
Endogenous variables								
Sale value ratio	−1.03	−4***	0.55	1.42	0.41	2.77***	1.93	9.12***
Purchase ratio	−0.22	−0.15	1.51	1.11	0.43	0.83	0.02	0.03
Subaru subsidiary	52.72	0.51	49.21	0.4	67.15	0.91	96.80	0.94
Subaru parent	24.14	0.28	−110.78	−1.41	−84.26	−1.87*	−76.62	−1.39
Exogenous variables								
Subsidiary toyota	−24.49	−1.89*	4.98	0.35	−3.40	−0.34	7.96	0.62
Nissan	−62.34	−2.27**	0.41	0.01	−15.10	−0.61	−2.90	−0.07
Mitsubishi	−25.41	−1.15	7.62	0.47	−3.74	−0.47	1.95	0.19
Mazda	5.46	0.2	−38.04	−1.17	−4.88	−0.5	0.61	0.04
Isuzu	−12.26	−0.31	−35.68	−1.11	−23.87	−1.61	−20.06	−1.2
Daihatsu	8.87	0.65	−10.43	−0.62	−7.05	−0.85	−12.84	−1.24
Hino	7.71	0.47	−4.55	−0.23	−0.44	−0.05	−21.77	−1.87*
Honda	−38.28	−2.41**	−15.45	−0.81	−10.71	−1.12	−2.79	−0.21
Parent Toyota	1.01	0.25	−4.79	−1.25	−13.48	−3.79***	−16.18	−4.4***
Nissan	−2.80	−0.12	28.39	1.35	13.63	1.3	12.52	0.96
Mitsubishi	3.51	0.23	−18.57	−1.27	−7.38	−1.3	−4.51	−0.61
Mazda	−16.75	−0.42	52.37	1.5	25.89	1.35	27.37	1.2
Isuzu	0.54	0.02	23.37	1.23	25.26	2.44**	18.92	1.57
Daihatsu	9.52	1.66*	0.25	0.03	21.32	4.14***	17.12	2.5**
Hino	7.86	0.29	−32.73	−1.4	−14.05	−1.27	−12.81	−0.94
Honda	−2.48	−0.09	33.98	1.28	20.31	1.67*	12.19	0.78

3.5 Conclusion

This chapter considered the Asanuma hypothesis on the technology cooperation association from the property rights theory, especially a general setup of Whinston (2003). Participation in the associations should be considered as non–contractible investments for the relation-specific skill. Does the Asanuma hypothesis hit the nail on the head? Which type of the PRT model fits the Japanese auto-parts suppliers? Are there any positive roles of the associations for knowledge sharing in "the hold-up problem?" The simplified models provide differential implications with respect to the comparative statics concerning the effects on vertical integration. Comparisons of the qualitative implications with our Tobit and IV Tobit regressions led to a conclusion. Yes, the Asanuma hypothesis turns out to be true. The model of exogenous acquisition of the relation-specific skill, or the model of a seller's self-investment for the relation-specific skill would be applicable to auto-parts procurement in Japan. Some associations find it a place to make non-contractible investments, while others may not. As Asanuma (1989, 1992) once insisted, the Japanese auto-parts industry is still diversity-carrying.

References

Angrist, J. D. (2001). Estimation of limited dependent variable models with dummy endogenous regressors: Simple strategies for empirical practice. *Journal of Business & Economic Statistics, 19*(1), 2–28.

Asanuma, B. (1989). Manufacturer-supplier relationships in Japan and the concept of relation-specific skill. *Journal of the Japanese & International Economies, 3*(1), 1–30.

Asanuma, B. (1992). Japanese manufacturer-supplier relationships in international perspective. In P. Sheard (Ed.), International adjustment and the Japanese economy. St. Leonards, Australia: Allen& Unwin, 99–124.

Hart, O. (1995). *Firms contracts and financial structure*. Oxford University Press.

Hart, O., & Moore, J. (1990). Property rights and the nature of the firm. *Journal of Political Economy, 98*(6), 1119–1158.

Hidalgo, C. (2015). *Why information grows: The evolution of order, from atoms to economies*. Basic Books.

Holmström, B., & Roberts, J. (1998). The boundaries of the firm revisited. *Journal of Economic Perspectives, 12*(4), 73–94.

Kiyotaki, N., & Moore, J. (1997). Credit cycles. *Journal of Political Economy, 105*(2), 211–248.

Lafontaine, F., & Slade, M. E. (2013). Inter-firm contracts: Evidence. In R. Gibbons & J. Roberts (Eds.), Handbook of organizational economics. Princeton & Oxford: Princeton University Press, 958–1013.

Lewbel, A., Dong, Y., & Yang, T. T. (2012). Comparing features of convenient estimators for binary choice models with endogenous regressors. *Canadian Journal of Economics/revue Canadienne D'économique, 45*(3), 809–829.

Milgrom, P., & Roberts, J. (1992). *Economics, organization & management*. Prentice Hall.

Newey, W. K. (1987). Efficient estimation of limited dependent variable models with endogenous explanatory variables. *Journal of Econometrics, 36*(3), 231–250.
Segal, I., & Whinston, M. D. (2013). Property rights. In R. Gibbons & J. Roberts (Eds.), Handbook of organizational economics. Princeton & Oxford: Princeton University Press, 100–158.
Whinston, M. D. (2003). On the transaction cost determinants of vertical integration. *Journal of Law, Economics, & Organization, 19*(1), 1–23.

Chapter 4
Automobile Electronics and Capital Adjustment Costs

Contents

Abstract To make quantitative evaluations on the nature of capital adjustment costs, in the face of technological changes, we estimate capital adjustment cost functions, either convex/non-convex, or irreversible (Cooper and Haltiwanger, Review of Economic Studies 73:611–633, 2006). A simulated method of moments is applied to the Bellman equations at an establishment level of Japanese auto-parts suppliers (*Census of Manufactures*), where experiencing a technological change of automobile electronics, an application of general purpose technology (David, American Economic Review 80:355–361, 1990; Jovanovic, B., & Rousseau, P. (2005). General purpose technologies. In Handbook of economic growth. vol. 1b P. Aghion & S. Durlauf (Eds.). Elsevier BV, 1181-1224.). Identifying when and where auto-electronics technologies have been embodied in auto-parts suppliers, we use patent acquisition data and plant products: electronically-controlled fuel injection; electric power steering; anti-lock brakes; airbags; navigation; wire harnesses; and lithium-ion batteries. For overall auto-parts suppliers, there are no adjustment costs in any

This chapter is based on Uchida, Takeda and Shirai "Technology and Capital Adjustment Costs: Micro evidence of automobile electronics in the auto-parts suppliers," RIETI Discussion Paper Series 12-E-001. We are grateful to Tsutomu Miyagawa, Naoki Shinada, Shin-ichi Fukuda, Hidehiko Ishihara, and the workshop participants for their helpful comments. We use micro data in the *Census of Manufacturers* and price data in the *Japan Industrial Productivity Database 2010* (JIP Database 2010). We appreciate the availability of both data sources. This chapter is financially supported by Grant-in-Aid for Scientific Research.

Y. Takeda and I. Uchida, *Information Agglomeration of Japanese Auto Parts Suppliers*,
https://doi.org/10.1007/978-981-19-3300-4_4

form, neither convex/non-convex, nor irreversible. As for the sectoral plants with automobile electronics embodied in the tangible capitals, we clearly detect a significant existence of the convex adjustment costs. Anomalously, auto electronics also make investment decisions reversible. Moreover, the fixed costs of plant restructuring, worker retraining, or organizational restructuring emerge, especially in the form of costs proportional to plant size rather than the opportunity cost of investment. The nature of adjustment costs implies economic policy measures to compensate for output losses arising from capital adjustment costs in the face of general purpose technologies.

Keywords Capital adjustment cost · General purpose technology · Automobile electronics · Simulated method of moments

4.1 Introduction

Regarding an outcome of research and development held by constructors and suppliers of newly-required parts, we witness a change in a trend of market prices for both automobiles and auto parts (Fig. 4.1). The fluctuation in prices happened parallelly for both, with the relative prices holding relatively steady till 1995. During the second half of the nineties, however, motor vehicles encountered a spike in prices, which remained on a gradual upward trend thereafter. By contrast, prices of auto parts and accessories constantly decreased from the mid-eighties. The structural change in the relative prices of auto parts coincides with the prominent rise of automobile electronics.

In view of the development in automobile electronics, this chapter considers a role of capital adjustment costs in lowering transaction costs associated with organizational links for information agglomeration, as introduced in Chap. 1 and Hidalgo (2015). In particular, what type of capital adjustment costs did automobile electronics raise in auto-parts suppliers? On the specific questions, this chapter sheds light from the standpoint of "general purpose technologies" (GPT; David, 1990; Jovanovic & Rousseau, 2005), exemplified by the invention of electricity and computer. As is well recognized from the variety of products we derive benefits from[1], automobile electronics makes full use of GPT. It is likely that GPT requires auto-parts suppliers to learn from capital-embodied technological progress, as the literature "investment-specific technology shocks" on adjustment costs suggests (for instance, Hornstein & Krusell, 1996). Are the capital adjustment costs associated with auto

[1] We can list the products here: engine control; electro AT (automatic transmission)/CVT (continuously variable transmission); electronically-controlled suspension; ABS (antilock brake system); train control system; electronically-controlled 4WS (4-wheel steering); EPS (electronically-controlled power steering); airbag; corner- and back-SONAR (sound navigation and ranging); driver positional memory; ACC (fully-automatic climate control system); cruise control; RKE (remote keyless entry); navigation; digital meters; multiplex transmission; on-board ETC (electronic toll collection); in-car camera; NVD (night vision device); or tire-pressure monitoring system.

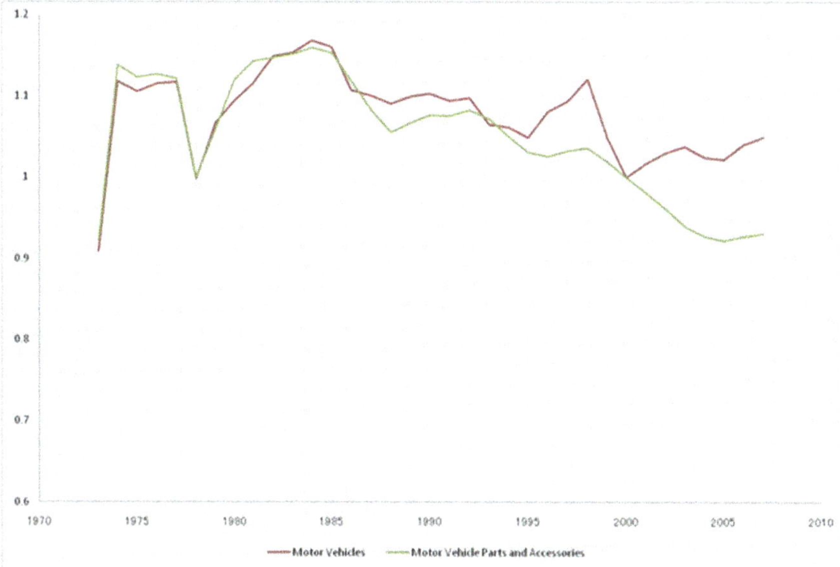

Fig. 4.1 Market prices of motor vehicles and motor vehicle parts and accessories; 1 in 2000; *Source* The Japan Industrial Productivity Database 2010 (JIP Database 2010)

electronics higher? We quantitatively explore the effect of automobile electronics on capital adjustment costs, as reviewed in Sect. 1.2.3 of Chap. 1, considering the nature of each type of adjustment costs with convex/non-convex or irreversible functions (Cooper & Haltiwanger, 2006).

Following Cooper and Haltiwanger (2006), we estimate via the simulated method of moments the Bellman equations for plants' dynamic optimization with respect to tangible capital, where there are decisions of inaction, buy, or sell capitals to choose discretely. Our main results suggest, though the estimates show a lack of stability in the coefficients related to adjustment costs, that the effects of automobile electronics are mixed, if any. For the overall sample of auto-parts suppliers, there are no adjustment costs in any form, neither convex/non-convex, nor irreversible. As for the sectoral plants where automobile electronics seems embodied in the tangible capitals, we clearly detect a significant existence of convex adjustment costs. Regarding another type of adjustment costs, on the one hand, the sell price of used capitals is anomalously higher than the buy price, which means auto electronics makes the investment decision reversible; on the other hand, the fixed costs of plant restructuring, worker retraining, or organizational restructuring emerge, especially in the form of costs proportional to the plant size rather than an opportunity cost of investment. The nature of adjustment costs associated with auto electronics implies economic policy measures that should be taken in order to compensate for the output losses from capital adjustment costs in the face of general purpose technologies.

The chapter is organized as follows: Section 4.2 describes our plant-level data of Japanese auto-parts suppliers (*Census of Manufactures*), where tangible capitals are measured, including the retirements for each plant. Among the items listed in the plant-level data, we can make use of each plant's products, a few of which embody developments in automobile electronics, an application of general purpose technology. According to another data source of the patent grant, we can identify when and where the embodied technological changes have been engineered owing to automobile electronics. Section 4.3 presents a structural estimation of plants' dynamic profit maximization, including either convex/non-convex, or irreversible adjustment cost functions (Cooper & Haltiwanger, 2006), as well as the overall sample of Japanese auto-parts suppliers. We also apply the structural estimation to partial sample plants identified as embodiments of automobile electronics. We compare the nature of capital adjustment costs between the overall sample and sectoral cases. Finally, we conclude with Sect. 4.4.

4.2 Plant-Level Data of the Japanese Auto-Parts Suppliers

Let us describe the data we use for estimation. The plant-level data are from the *Census of Manufactures* compiled by the Ministry of Economy, Trade and Industry, Japan. We treat two sub-groups classified as automotive body and concomitant (classification number 3012) and automotive component and accessory (number 3013).[2]

4.2.1 Capital Retirement

We consider total tangible capitals, including these categories: establishment and structure; machinery and equipment; and ship, vehicle, transport equipment, etc. We exclude land as the capital we use since it does not seem that for a unit of each plant, land expansion and contraction can be an adjustment mean, except in plant opening or closing.[3] Data on capital retirements are available for our tangible capitals. Here we define capital stocks at the beginning of the period, following the perpetual inventory method:

---

[2] The classification number has been changed in 1985, 2002, and 2008.

[3] In consideration of simultaneity in decision-makings between the tangible capitals and land, we will use the latter as an instrumental variable in estimating the profit function where the tangible capitals are one of the determinants. Nominal land capital is deflated with the Urban Land Price Index of six large city areas (Japan Real Estate Institute).

Capital stock at the beginning of the period: $K_{t-1} = I_t + (1 - \delta)K_t$
Net investment during the period: $I_t = EXP_t - RET_t$
Gross expenditures: EXP_t
Gross retirements: RET_t

With regard to how to handle the book value, we follow an equation that retired capitals RET_t is equal to current changes in tangible fixed assets, minus remaining book values of retired tangible fixed assets multiplied by market-book value ratios.[4]

The physical depreciation rate δ is 0.073034 for 1986–1992 and 0.09593197 for 1993–2007, considering a change in the depreciation rates probably due to higher obsolescence speed or higher shares of software in capital stocks.[5] The deflators for capital category, excluding land, are ratios of nominal investment matrix to real one in JIP2010: number 33 (non-residential construction) for establishment and structure; 7 (general industrial machinery, including materials handling equipment), 10 (chemical machinery), 11 (metalworking machines), 13 (special industrial machinery), 21 (electricity transmission and distribution apparatus), 22 (electric lighting fixtures and apparatus) for machinery and equipment; and others (32 capital goods) for ship, vehicle, transport equipment, etc.

We omit some outlier samples with either negative levels of capital K_{it} or anomalous values of investment rate $i_{it} \equiv \frac{I_{it}}{K_{it}}$ at the top and bottom 1% of the distribution. Summary statistics is extracted with regard to investment rate in Table 4.1. Of the overall sample, inactive plants with $I_{it} = 0$ occupy about 7%. There is a positively skewed distribution with the positive (higher than 0.2) spikes even more frequent than the negative (lower than 0.2)—the lumpiness and asymmetry that would lead fixed adjustment costs and irreversibility—in later estimation. Our data (the *Census of Manufactures*) provide us with a serial correlation 0.0305 of the investment rates, lower than 0.058 in Cooper and Haltiwanger (2006) data (the *Longitudinal Research Database*). The more lumpy capital adjustments also seem to lead the dominance of the non-convex adjustment cost function.

4.2.2 Identification of Auto-Electronics Technologies

To identify the effects of electronics on capital adjustment costs, we measure some dummy variables representing the products that plants manufacture to benefit from electronic technologies, and when electronic technologies are embodied in the

[4] In terms of how to handle the book values, we try to construct retired capitals in two other ways besides the one described in the text (Tonogi et al., 2010). In one method, retired capitals are equal to current changes in tangible fixed assets, minus remaining book values of retired tangible fixed assets for the period. The other deals only with the current changes in tangible fixed assets. In these two cases, there are some anomalous results in estimations; so we do not adopt those capital retirements.

[5] We have an alternative of the physical depreciation rates 0 for land, 0.05640 for establishment and structure, 0.09489 for machinery and equipment, 0.147 for ship, vehicle, transport equipment, etc.

Table 4.1 Summary statistics (1): Investment rates in the overall sample

Period: 1986–2007	Tangible capital
Average investment rate	0.1699
Inaction rate	0.069
Fraction of observations with negative investment	0.0536
Spike rate: positive, higher than 0.2	0.2937
Spike rate: negative, lower than –0.2	0.00395
Serial correlation Corr (i_{it}, i_{it-1})	0.0305
Correlation w/profitability Corr (i_{it}, a_t)	0.1376

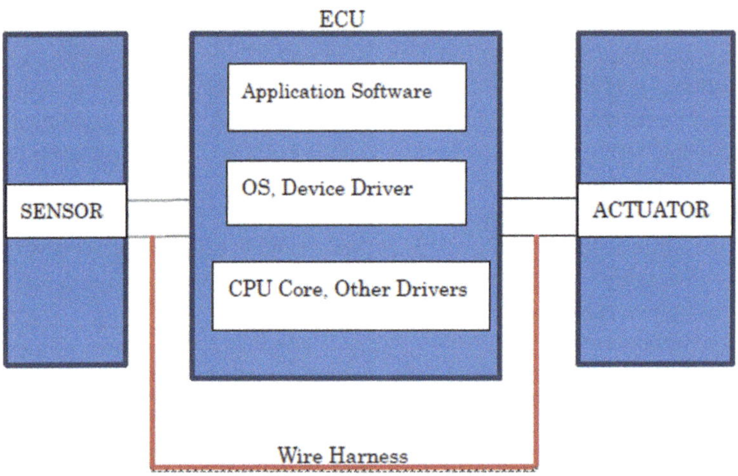

Fig. 4.2 Automobile electronics; *Source* Fig. 2.1 in Tokuda and Saeki (2007b)

suppliers' capital stocks. Automobile electronics can be thought of as an application of information technology (IT), a GPT.

On the automobile electronics system, we rely on Tokuda and Saeki's (2007a, 2007b, 2007c) detailed description of the modularity and network of the technology.[6] We can decompose automobile electronics into four parts: sensor; electronic control unit (ECU); actuator; and wire harness. As Fig. 4.2 conceptually shows, electronics can be compared with human anatomy, where the five senses cognize the environment (corresponding to sensor)—the brain transfers signals from the five senses to the muscle (ECU), limb muscles respond to the signals from the brain (actuator), and nerves and vessels connect between the senses and muscles (wire harness). The four parts consist of each market shared by auto-parts companies as well as the major electric equipment companies. As is seen in the computer industry, compatibility standardization might lead to network externality between each product.

[6] The description covers quite usefully the history and the market shares of the suppliers.

Among all the systems used for automobiles, according to Tokuda and Saeki (2007c), we classify the following products as electronics: electronically-controlled fuel injection device (PET); electric power steering (EPS); anti-lock brake system (ABS); airbags; navigation system; wire harness; and lithium-ion battery. We also identify periods when GPT is innovatively associated with the technologies listed above, with the number of patents hit by each keyword in the *Patent Licensing Information Database.*

4.2.2.1 Product Dummies

Regarding where automobile electronic technologies are embodied, we draw on a document of Tokuda and Saeki (2007c), which describes the main systems for automobile electronics: electronically-controlled fuel injection device (PET); electric power steering (EPS); anti-lock brake system (ABS); airbags; and navigation system. In addition to the five main systems associated with automobile electronics, we reckon two more products: wire harness and lithium-ion battery.

Although our criteria for product dummy variables are far from perfect, each system can be interpreted as corresponding to the following commodity indices in the *Census of Manufactures*: parts, attachments, and accessories of internal combustion engines for motor vehicles (#311314) for PET; parts of driving, transmission, and operating units (#311315) for EPS[7]; parts of suspension and brake systems (#311316) for ABS; parts of chassis and bodies (#311317) for airbags; radio-applied equipment (#301315) for navigation system; parts, attachments, and accessories of auxiliary equipment for internal combustion engines (#292221) for wire harness; and lithium-ion batteries (#295113).

4.2.2.2 Time-Dummies for Patent Acquisitions

As for the identification of the time periods when the electronics system was embodied, a criterion we adopt is based on the number of patents for each product associated with the electronic technologies. We additionally use a database in the *Industrial Property Digital Library*, which offers free online access to IP Gazettes of the Japan Patent Office (JPO).[8]

Among the databases on intellectual properties submitted to JPO, the Patent Gazettes and Unexamined Patent Application Gazettes provide data on the number of patent grants and patent applications, respectively, in Japanese with either keywords, issue dates, or so on. The Patent Gazettes cover searchable issue dates starting 1986 and the Unexamined Patent Application Gazettes starting 1993.

We choose the time periods when many patent grant cases are available in the JPO data, depicted in Figures 4.3, 4.4, 4.5, 4.6, 4.7, 4.8 and 4.9. In the case of PET,

---

[7] It includes the automatic transmission (AT) technologies.

[8] It is publicly available from http://www.ipdl.inpit.go.jp/homepg_c.ipdl.

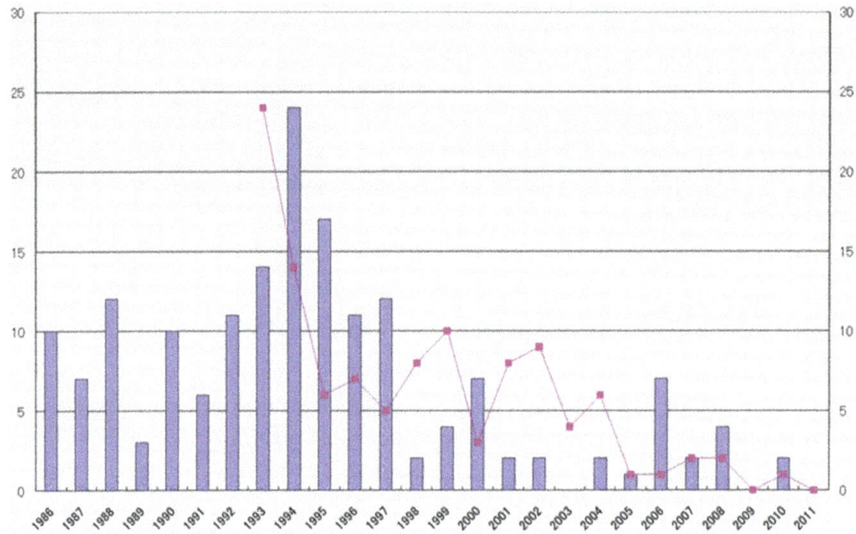

Fig. 4.3 The number of patent acquisitions (vertical Bar; left axis) and applications (solid line; right axis), as of July 8, 2011: electronically-controlled fuel injection device (PET); *Source* Industrial Property Digital Library

the time dummy variable takes the value 1 from 1986 to 1997, or 0 otherwise; the number of observations is 6,733. The time dummy variable for EPS is 1 for 1999–2007 (number of observations 4,912); for ABS 2001–2007 (number of observations 2031); for airbags 1998–2007 (number of observations 5,086); for wire harness 1999–2007 (number of observations 108); for lithium-ion battery 2000 to 2007 (number of observations is 0)[9]; and for navigation system 1997–2007 (number of observations 17).

Note that our choice of the time dummy variables is based on casual observations of the number of patent grants identified with the product keywords above.[10] To show comparability of our time dummy variables with estimates a_{it} on productivity changes incurred by a plant i classified into ones with electronic innovations at a period t, we estimate correlation ratios η between the time dummy variable and productivity changes (t-statistics in parenthesis): −0.0797(−8.67) for PET time dummy variable; 0.0366(3.65) for EPS time dummy variable; 0.0567(4.26) for ABS time dummy variable; −0.0011(−0.11) for airbag time dummy variable; 0.0746(0.99) for the wire harness time dummy variable; and 0.3004(1.47) for the navigation time dummy variable. Among the time dummies we use, the statistical significance suggests that

[9] We confirm that our sample includes a plant of a well-known company as a pioneering producer of lithium-ion battery, but the plant does not list its products in the *Census of Manufactures* survey.

[10] Some previous research that uses count data in patent applications, grants, and citations is surveyed in Griliches (1990); more recent examples include Griffith et al. (2006), or Bloom et al. (2007).

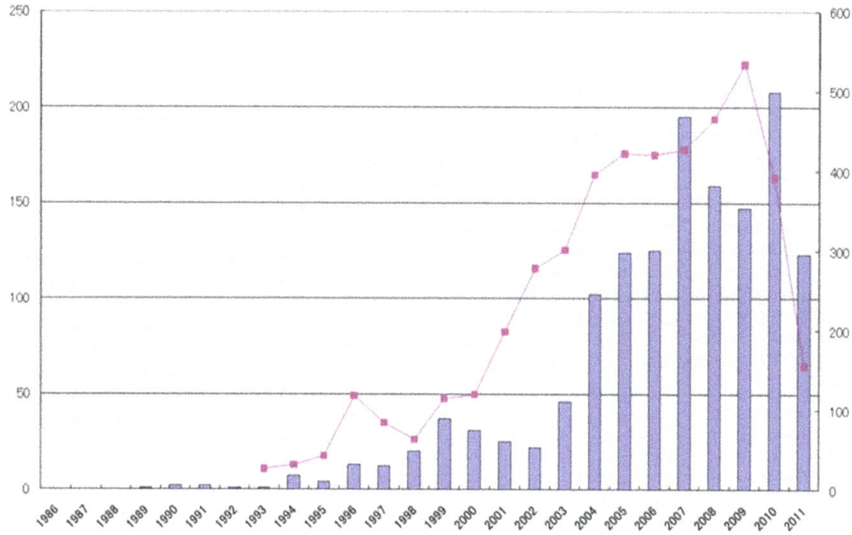

Fig. 4.4 The number of patent acquisitions (vertical Bar; left axis) and applications (solid line; right axis), as of July 8, 2011: electric power steering (EPS); *Source* Industrial Property Digital Library

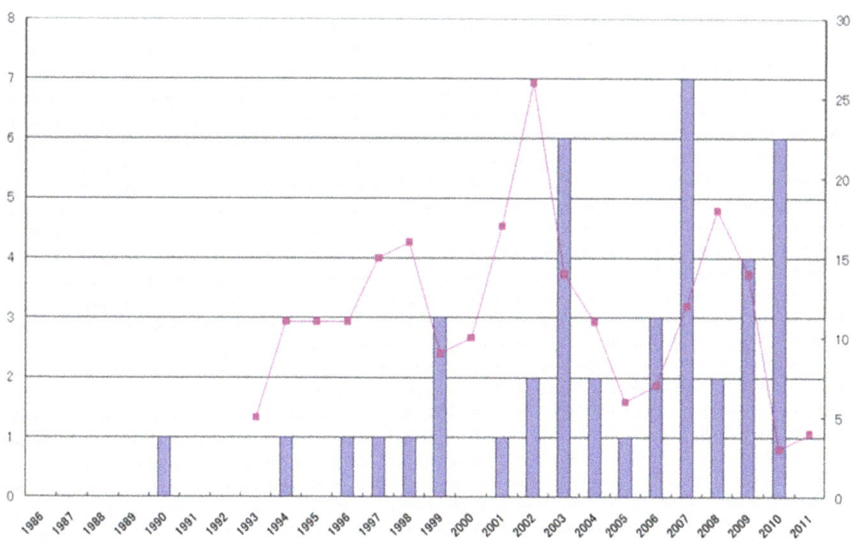

Fig. 4.5 The number of patent acquisitions (vertical Bar; left axis) and applications (solid line; right axis), as of July 8, 2011: anti-lock brake system (ABS); *Source* Industrial Property Digital Library

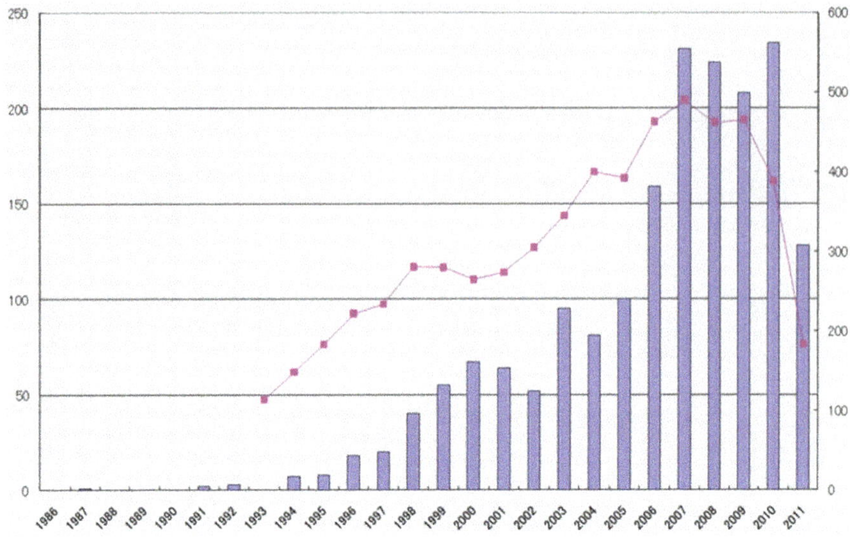

Fig. 4.6 The number of patent acquisitions (vertical Bar; left axis) and applications (solid line; right axis), as of July 8, 2011: airbag; *Source* Industrial Property Digital Library

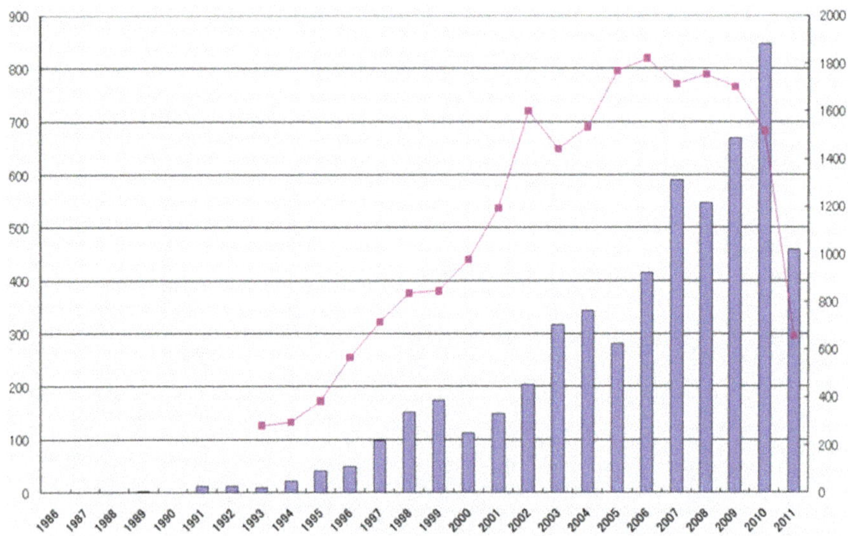

Fig. 4.7 The number of patent acquisitions (vertical Bar; left axis) and applications (solid line; right axis), as of July 8, 2011: navigation system; *Source* Industrial Property Digital Library

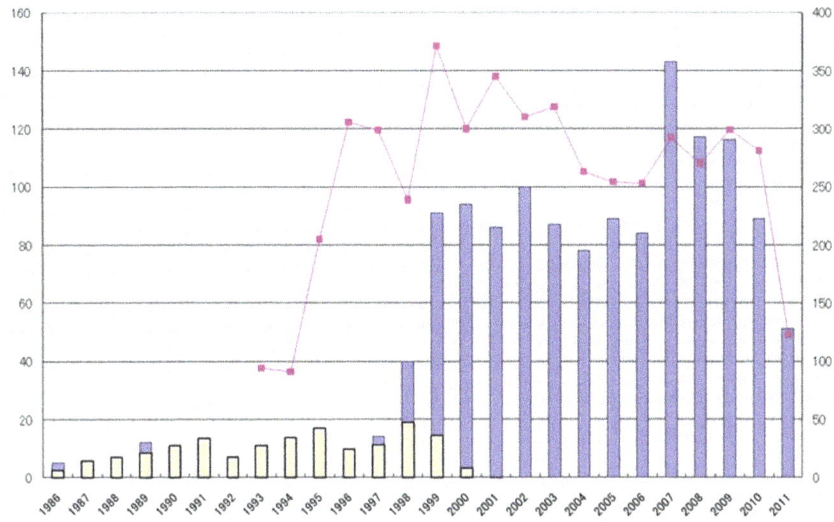

Fig. 4.8 The number of patent acquisitions (vertical Bar; left axis) and applications (solid line; right axis), as of July 8, 2011: wire harness; *Source* Industrial Property Digital Library

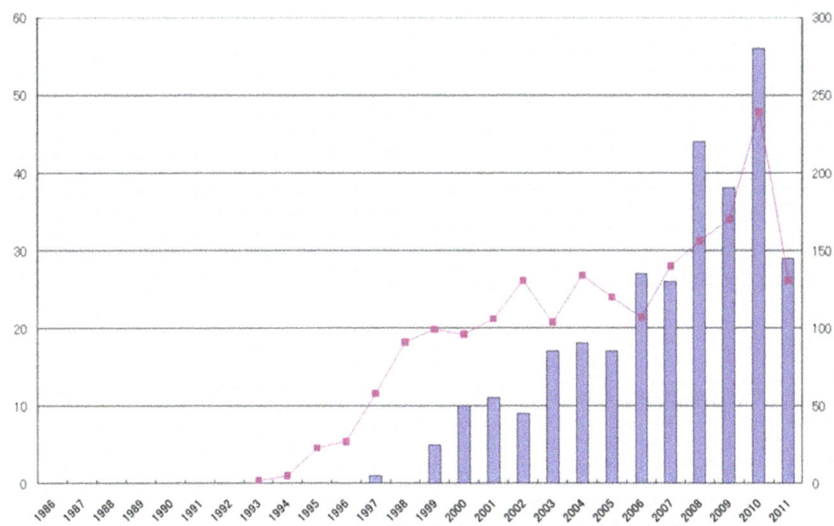

Fig. 4.9 The number of patent acquisitions (vertical Bar; left axis) and applications (solid line; right axis), as of July 8, 2011: lithium-ion battery; *Source* Industrial Property Digital Library

the EPS and ABS time dummy variables are better indicators of automobile electronic technologies.

4.3 Estimation

We draw on the specifications of the functions by Cooper and Haltiwanger (2006). Suppose a production function of the constant-return-to-scale Cobb-Douglas type $y = AK^{\alpha}L^{1-\alpha}$ and an inverse demand function for the plant's products with constant price-elasticity $p = y^{-\eta}$. It is a profit function $\Pi = R(y) - \omega L$ to be maximized with respect to a variable factor of production L (labor inputs), where ω is a wage rate and the revenue function is $R(y) = py = \left(AK^{\alpha}L^{1-\alpha}\right)^{1-\eta}$. The static profit maximization leads to a labor demand function

$$L = (1-\eta)^{-\frac{1}{(1-\alpha)(1-\eta)-1}} A^{-\frac{1-\eta}{(1-\alpha)(1-\eta)-1}} \omega^{\frac{1}{(1-\alpha)(1-\eta)-1}} K^{-\frac{\alpha(1-\eta)}{(1-\alpha)(1-\eta)-1}}$$

and the indirect profit function

$$\Pi(A,\omega,K) = (1-\eta)^{-\frac{(1-\alpha)(1-\eta)}{(1-\alpha)(1-\eta)-1}} \eta A^{-\frac{1-\eta}{(1-\alpha)(1-\eta)-1}} \omega^{\frac{(1-\alpha)(1-\eta)}{(1-\alpha)(1-\eta)-1}} K^{-\frac{\alpha(1-\eta)}{(1-\alpha)(1-\eta)-1}}$$

Summarizing the coefficients in the profit function, we denote

$$\boldsymbol{\Pi(A_{it}, K_{it}) = A_{it}K_{it}^{\theta}} \tag{4.1}$$

where $A_{it} \equiv (1-\eta)^{-\frac{(1-\alpha)(1-\eta)}{(1-\alpha)(1-\eta)-1}} \eta A^{-\frac{1-\eta}{(1-\alpha)(1-\eta)-1}} \omega^{\frac{(1-\alpha)(1-\eta)}{(1-\alpha)(1-\eta)-1}}$ and $\theta \equiv -\frac{\alpha(1-\eta)}{(1-\alpha)(1-\eta)-1}$. Intuitively speaking, the more perfect the price competition in a product market (i.e., the smaller a positive value of η near zero), the higher the value of θ in physical capital K in the profit function.

4.3.1 Functional Forms of Adjustment Cost

4.3.1.1 Convex/Non-Convex

Now we incorporate adjustment costs into a dynamic optimization problem. The conventional functional form of the capital adjustment cost assumes convexity. Under conditions of constant-return-to-scale function of adjustment costs with respect to investment and capital stock, Hayashi (1982) shows an equivalence of the average and the marginal Tobin's q in a perfect capital market. The form is

$$\boldsymbol{C(I, A, K)} = \frac{\gamma}{2}\left(\frac{I}{K}\right)^2 \boldsymbol{K} \tag{4.2}$$

where a parameter γ indicates the convexity of capital adjustment. The higher the value of γ, the smoother the capital adjustment is. In an extreme case of $\gamma = 0$ without any adjustment cost, the optimal investment rate will be very responsive to shocks affecting the first-order condition of profit-maximizing agents.

However, the capital adjustment cost function is also built on non-convexity, capturing the existence of fixed costs. The fixed costs are considered as stemming from plant restructuring, worker retraining, or organizational restructuring. These costs reflect indivisibilities in capital; increasing returns to the installation of new capital; and increasing returns to retraining and restructuring of production activities. A functional form of such non-convex adjustment costs can be specified in the Bellman equation for profit maximization as,

$$\boldsymbol{V(A,K) = max\left\{V^i(A,K),\, V^a(A,K)\right\}} \tag{4.3}$$

$$V^i(A,K) = \Pi(A,K) + \beta E_{A'|A} V\left(A', K(1-\delta)\right)$$

$$V^a(A,K) = \max_I \Pi(A,K)\lambda - FK - pI + \beta E_{A'|A} V\left(A', K'\right)$$

where either active investment $V^a(A,K)$ or inactivity $V^i(A,K)$ is chosen discretely.

In the active case, there are two types of capital adjustment costs. One is an opportunity cost $\lambda < 1$ of investment, which means a fall in plant productivity by a factor of $1 - \lambda$ of profits; the other type of adjustment cost F depends on the level of capital K in a fixed way proportional to the size of the plant.

4.3.1.2 Irreversibility

There is another possibility of transaction costs that reflects the differentials between the buying and selling price of capital. The transaction costs are probably caused by capital specificity or asymmetric information between buyers and sellers. We assume

$$\boldsymbol{p(I) = \begin{cases} p_b & if \quad I > 0 \\ p_s & if \quad I < 0 \end{cases}} \tag{4.4}$$

where $p_b \geq p_s$. The gap between buying and selling prices will create an inaction region for the plants.

Then the value function of the plants is given by

$$\boldsymbol{V(A,K)= max\{V^b(A,K), V^s(A,K), V^i(A,K)\}} \tag{4.5}$$

$$V^b(A,K) = \max_I \Pi(A,K) - p_b I + \beta E_{A'|A} V\big(A', K(1-\delta)+I\big)$$

$$V^s(A,K) = \max_R \Pi(A,K) + p_s R + \beta E_{A'|A} V\big(A', K(1-\delta)I - R\big)$$

$$V^i(A,K) = \Pi(A,K) + \beta E_{A'|A} V\big(A', K(1-\delta)\big)$$

where purchase of new capital I, retirement of old capital R, and inaction of neither investment nor retirement are distinguished with respect to irreversible decision-making.

4.3.2 Auxiliary Estimation of Productivity Processes

We will take two-step estimations for the Bellman equation of plants' profit optimization problem. In Step 1 as an auxiliary estimation, we estimate a plant's profit function, which depends on productivity shocks consisting of an aggregate common shock and plant-specific one. We apply a dynamic panel-data estimation of system GMM (Blundell & Bond, 1998). Following a Tauchen (1986) procedure for discretizing the autoregressive process of order 1 AR(1) based on the estimates of productivity processes, in Step 2 we apply a simulated method of moments (SMM) to the Bellman equation of plants' profit maximization, focusing on the parameters in the capital adjustment cost functions.

In the estimated equation, we make use of a decomposition of a logged productivity $a_{it} = \log A_{it}$ into an aggregate common shock b_t and a plant-specific shock ε_{it}:

$$\boldsymbol{b_t= \mu_b+\rho_b b_{t-1}+\eta_{bt}} \tag{4.6}$$

We assume each component follows different AR(1) time-series processes,

$$\boldsymbol{b_t= \mu_b+\rho_b b_{t-1}+\eta_{bt}} \tag{4.7}$$

$$\varepsilon_{it} = \rho_\varepsilon \varepsilon_{it-1} + \eta_{it}$$

where standard deviations of the innovations η_{bt} and η_{it} are σ_b and σ_ε, respectively. We estimate an equation

$$\boldsymbol{\pi_{it}= \rho_\varepsilon \pi_{it-1}+\theta k_{it}-\rho_\varepsilon \theta k_{t-1}+b_t-\rho_\varepsilon b_{t-1}+\eta_{it}} \tag{4.8}$$

to which we apply the GMM system of Blundell and Bond (1998). We choose options of two-step efficient estimation with estimated robust standard errors (Windmeijer, 2005; Roodman, 2006). Along with GMM-type instruments π_{it-2}, k_{it-1}, and k_{t-2}, we use current and lagged real values of land capital, both of which seem to be highly correlated with the tangible capital. To capture the effects of the aggregate common shock, we also use current and lagged levels of logged real GDP and current and lagged log-prices of intermediate inputs and labors relative to product price, as well as a comprehensive list of time dummy variables.

The number of observations is 33,092 for 1986 to 2007. The profit is defined as real values equal to revenues minus a sum of total cash wages and material amount used. The Arellano and Bond (1991) test for AR(1) of the error term shows a z-value of 1.48 with a probability value of 0.138, that is an acceptance of a null hypothesis of no serial correlation. The Hansen J test of overidentifying restrictions and difference-in-Hansen tests of exogeneity of instrument subsets also cannot reject the validity of instruments. As Table 4.2 shows, the estimates of the AR(1) coefficient ρ_ε on the idiosyncratic shock ε_{it} are 0.689 (standard error 0.039). As for the parameter θ in the profit function, the estimates indicate 0.60 (S.E. 0.13). The standard deviations of the idiosyncratic shock η_{it} as the residual term in the equation is 0.146.

Next, we recover the aggregate common shock b_t in the following way: the productivity a_{it} is calculated with the estimates of a parameter θ in the profit function; and the aggregate shock b_t is the mean of the productivity a_{it} in each year over the plants. We estimate AR(1) with a constant term process of the aggregate shock using OLS. The AR(1) coefficient ρ_b (standard error) and the standard deviation of the error η_{bt} term are 0.73 (0.17) and 0.086, respectively. The estimated constant is 1.29 (0.81), stochastically insignificant in Table 4.3.

The estimated productivity a_{it} is also correlated with investment rates, the correlation coefficient 0.1376. For both AR(1) processes of the productivity shock a_{it}, we apply an approximating method for a first-order Markov process (Tauchen, 1986; Tauchen & Hussey, 1991). The number of aggregate and idiosyncratic states are set equal to 3 and 10, respectively.

Table 4.2 System GMM estimates of profit function (1): the overall sample

Variables	Coef.	Corrected Std. Err.	Z
π_{it-1}	0.689	0.039	17.78
k_{it}	0.60	0.13	4.73
k_{t-1}	–0.43	0.15	–2.91
Log-real GDP_t	–32.96	11.94	–2.76
Log-real GDP_{t-1}	33.13	11.96	2.77
Log-inter. input $price_t$	–43.28	17.29	–2.50
Log-inter. input $price_{t-1}$	–85.25	31.297	–2.72
Log-$wage_t$	–25.56	9.77	–2.62
Log-$wage_{t-1}$	46.77	17.86	2.62

Table 4.3 Key parameters in profit function (1): the overall sample

	Constant(S.E.)	AR(1)(S.E.)	
ε_{it}	–	ρ_ε: 0.689(0.039)	$\mathrm{Std}(\eta_{it}) = \sigma_\varepsilon$: 0.146
b_t	1.29(0.81)	ρ_b: 0.73 (0.17)	$\mathrm{Std}(\eta_{bt}) = \sigma_b$: 0.086
a_{it}			$\mathrm{Corr}(a_{it}, i_{it}) = 0.1376$

4.3.3 *Simulated Method of Moments for Adjustment Cost Functions*

Simulated method of moments is applied to our data, where we find a parameter vector $\Theta = (F, \lambda, p_s, \gamma)$ minimizing a weighted distance between empirical and simulated moments as follows:

$$\min_{\Theta} J(\Theta) = \left[\Psi^d - \Psi^S(\Theta)\right]' W \left[\Psi^d - \Psi^S(\Theta)\right] \tag{4.9}$$

where we assume a parameter p_b set at 1. In the first step, given Θ, we execute a value function iteration for the Bellman equation (4.3) or (4.5). The resulting policy function, in the second step, generates a panel data set of the endogenous variables. In the third step, the panel data obtains $\Psi^S(\Theta)$. Finally, in the fourth step, a minimization of $J(\Theta)$ with some weighting matrix W is done with respect to Θ. The empirical moments we should match with the minimization are inaction rates, two spike rates, positive (higher than 0.2) and negative (lower than –0.2), serial correlation of the investment rates $\mathrm{Corr}(i_{it}, i_{it-1})$, and correlation of the investment rates with profitability $\mathrm{Corr}(a_{it}, i_{it})$. We also set the annual discount rate β at 0.95 and the annual rate of depreciation δ at 0.08031, a simple average of the rates we used in the perpetual inventory method, 0.073034 for 1986–1992 and 0.09593197 for 1993–2007. The practical minimization procedure is based on the Fackler and Tastan (2008) program code, which provides a general framework for simulation based on the indirect inference methodology. We use the Matlab optimization routine *fminsearch* for optimization algorithm.

Table 4.4 indicates the coefficients on the adjustment cost parameters, their asymptotic standard errors and t-statistics. Though the simulated moments are inadequately matched with the sample moments, the parameter estimates suggest a fact that convex adjustment cost is insignificant, fixed costs are none since a parameter F is insignificant and a parameter λ is not different from 1, and irreversibility is also none since $p_s = 1 = p_b$. That is, there are no adjustment costs, neither convex/non-convex, nor irreversible.

Table 4.4 SMM Estimates of the Bellman Equation (1): the overall sample

Parameters	Coef.	ASE(t-stat)
F	–0.0063	0.0079(–0.7952)
Γ	0.0741	0.1296(0.5718)
Ps	1.0168	0.0182(55.9738)
Λ	1.0373	0.1657(6.2601)
Moments	Sample	Simulation
$\text{Corr}(i_{it}, i_{it-1})$	0.0305	0.4995
$\text{Corr}(i_{it}, a_{it})$	0.1376	0.0104
Positive spike rate	0.2937	0.1529
Negative spike rate	0.00395	0.0111
Inaction rate	0.069	0

4.3.4 Effects of Automobile Electronics on Adjustment Costs

We take some sectoral cases as the samples of plants with embodied technological progress engineered by automobile electronics. We assume that a sample of the plants benefitting from auto electronics might probably possess a different productivity process of A in the profit function $\Pi(A, K)$.

Among all the combinations of each products PET, EPS, ABS, AB, WH, LI, or NV, four samples are represented:(PET ∪ EPS ∪ ABS ∪ AB ∪ WH ∪ LI ∪ NV); (EPS ∪ ABS); (EPS ∪ ABS ∪ WH); and (AB ∪ LI ∪ NV). The numbers of observations are 10,181, 3,507, 3,534, or 3,068, respectively.

Comparing with the coefficients in the benchmark case of the overall sample 2, we state some differences in the estimated parameters ρ_ε, ρ_b, and θ seen in Tables 4.5 and 4.6. In the case of (EPS ∪ ABS) or (EPS ∪ ABS ∪ WH), the estimated parameter θ in the profit function is higher than in the benchmark case, since it is likely that these core technologies of automobiles are publicly available through patent acquisitions. So the plants with the high technology or permission to use the applicable patents face quite a perfect competition in each product market, resulting in higher estimates of 0 of physical capital K. In another case of (AB ∪ LI ∪ NV) or (PET ∪ EPS ∪ ABS ∪ AB ∪ WH ∪ LI ∪ NV), where Japanese electric companies like Mitsubishi Electric Corporation gain market share taking advantage of the primary product development, the relatively lower price elasticity in the electric product markets leads to lower or insignificant coefficients of the parameter θ.

As for the AR(1) parameters ρ_ε and ρ_b of the idiosyncratic/aggregate productivity shown in Table 4.7, the core automobile technologies have a tendency of no serial correlations in the idiosyncratic ingredient, but high serial correlations in the aggregate one. In contrast, the electric products have a little lower serial correlation in the idiosyncratic productivity, with the aggregate one remaining almost the same.

Table 4.5 Summary statistics (2): Investment rates in sectoral C\cases

Period: 1986–2007	$PET \cup EPS \cup ABS \cup AB \cup WH \cup LI \cup NV$	$EPS \cup ABS$	$EPS \cup ABS \cup WH$	$AB \cup LI \cup NV$
Average investment rate	0.194	0.182	0.181	0.182
Inaction rate	0.058	0.049	0.048	0.066
Fraction of observations with negative investment	0.064	0.069	0.069	0.079
Spike rate: positive, higher than 0.2	0.325	0.303	0.304	0.3004
Spike rate: negative, lower than –0.2	0.008	0.0103	0.011	0.0104
Serial correlation $Corr(i_{it}, i_{it-1})$	0.059	0.0104	0.0105	0.0421
Correlation w/ profitability $Corr(i_{it}, a_{it})$	0.122	0.184	0.183	0.109

Table 4.6 System GMM estimates of profit function (2): Sectoral cases

Variables	$PET \cup EPS \cup ABS \cup AB \cup WH \cup LI \cup NV$	$EPS \cup ABS$	$EPS \cup ABS \cup WH$	$AB \cup LI \cup NV$
	Coef. (S.E;Z)			
π_{it-1}	0.62 (0.069;8.94)	0.43 (0.35;1.20)	0.43 (0.45;0.94)	0.599 (0.14;4.29)
k_{it}	0.48 (0.17;2.76)	0.81 (0.35;2.31)	0.81 (0.46;1.75)	0.25 (0.30;0.82)
k_{t-1}	–0.22 (0.18;–1.22)	–0.398 (0.22; –1.83)	–0.41 (0.29; –1.45)	0.038 (0.28;0.14)
Log-real GDP_t	–37.39 (18.75;–1.99)	–37.89 (54.65; –0.69)	–38.95 (66.45; –0.59)	–39.40 (37.18;–1.06)
Log-real GDP_{t-1}	37.55 (18.76;2.00)	38.09 (54.57;0.70)	39.16 (66.33;0.59)	39.57 (37.22;1.06)
Log-inter. inputs $price_t$	–52.18 (27.51;–1.90)	–55.23 (77.91; –0.71)	–56.67 (94.25;–0.60)	–53.61 (53.74;–1.00)
Log-inter. inputs $price_{t-1}$	–101.29 (49.16;–2.06)	–107.18 (150.86; –0.71)	–109.44 (184.30;–0.59)	–100.58 (99.30;–1.01)
Log-$wage_t$	–30.14 (15.39;–1.96)	–31.76 (47.17;-0.67)	–32.49 (57.69;–0.56)	–30.20 (30.55;–0.99)
Log-$wage_{t-1}$	55.59 (28.19;1.97)	58.83 (84.87;0.69)	60.21 (103.47;0.58)	55.81 (56.05;1.00)

Table 4.7 Key parameters in profit function (2): Sectoral cases

	Constant(S.E.)	AR(1)(S.E.)	
PET ∪ EPS ∪ ABS ∪ AB ∪ WH ∪ LI ∪ NV			
ε_{it}	–	ρ_ε:0.62(0.069)	$Std(\eta_{it}) = \sigma_\varepsilon$:0.379
b_t	1.54(0.93)	ρ_b:0.75(0.16)	$Std(\eta_{bt}) = \sigma_b$:0.078
a_{it}			$Corr(a_{it}, i_{it})$=0.293
EPS ∪ ABS			
ε_{it}	–	ρ_ε:0.43(0.35)	$Std(\eta_{it}) = \sigma_\varepsilon$:0.089
b_t	0.23(0.47)	ρ_b:0.92(0.19)	$Std(\eta_{bt}) = \sigma_b$:0.06
a_{it}			$Corr(a_{it}, i_{it})$=0.07
EPS ∪ ABS ∪ WH			
ε_{it}	–	ρ_ε:0.43(0.45)	$Std(\eta_{it}) = \sigma_\varepsilon$:0.089
b_t	0.25(0.42)	ρ_b:0.91(0.17)	$Std(\eta_{bt}) = \sigma_b$:0.06
a_{it}			$Corr(a_{it}, i_{it})$=0.06
AB ∪ LI ∪ NV			
ε_{it}	–	ρ_ε:0.599(0.14)	$Std(\eta_{it}) = \sigma_\varepsilon$:0.144
b_t	8.95(0.55)	ρ_b:–0.03(0.06)	$Std(\eta_{bt}) = \sigma_b$:0.11
a_{it}			$Corr(a_{it}, i_{it}) = 0.39$

Table 4.8 shows our SMM estimates. For the sectoral cases, we have to see some anomalous results. Note that, among the seven time-product dummies, the correlation ratios η between the dummy variables and productivity estimates a_{it} suggest that the variables EPS and ABS are appropriate for identifying the auto-electronic effects. Based on the appropriateness, we give more priority to cases of (EPS ∪ ABS)and(EPS ∪ ABS ∪ WH). Table 4.8 indicates that the effects of automobile electronics are mixed, if any. For the overall sample of auto-parts suppliers, there are no adjustment costs in any form, neither convex/non-convex, nor irreversible. As for the sectoral plants where automobile electronics seems embodied in the tangible capitals, we clearly detect a significant existence of the convex adjustment costs. Regarding another type of the adjustment costs, on the one hand, the sell price of the used capitals is anomalously higher than the buy price, which means auto electronics makes investment decision reversible; on the other hand, the fixed costs of plant restructuring, worker retraining, or organizational restructuring emerge, especially in the form of costs proportional to the plant size rather than an opportunity cost of investment.

Table 4.8 SMM estimates of the Bellman Equation (2): Sectoral cases

Parameters	*PET* ∪ *EPS* ∪ *ABS* ∪*AB* ∪ *WH* ∪ *LI* ∪ *NV*	*EPS* ∪ *ABS*	*EPS* ∪ *ABS* ∪ *WH*	*AB* ∪ *LI* ∪ *NV*
	Coef. (A.S.E; t–stat)			
F	–0.02357 (0.000057;–411.86)	0.0071 (0.0047;1.508)	0.0073 (0.000026;277.078)	–0.02196 (0.000000;–inf)
Γ	0.1769 (0.000066;2692.82)	0.0676 (2.556;0.026)	0.0720 (0.000000;inf)	0.1667 (0.000000;inf)
Ps	–0.769 (0.0000;–inf)	1.0104 (0.564;1.791)	1.0118 (0.00027;3713.86)	–1.3163 (0.000000;–inf)
Λ	0.8669 (0.000066;13192.43)	1.1759 (2.174;0.541)	1.1328 (0.000000;inf)	1.4173 (0.000000;inf)
Moments	Simulation (Sample)			
$Corr(i_{it}, i_{it-1})$	0.8060 (0.059)	0.9972 (0.0104)	0.9966 (0.0105)	0.9873 (0.0421)
$Corr(i_{it}, a_{it})$	0.0001 (0.122)	–0.0006 (0.184)	0.0037 (0.183)	0.0030 (0.109)
Positive spike rate	0.0260 (0.325)	0.1522 (0.303)	0.1346 (0.304)	0.0000 (0.3004)
Negative spike rate	0 (0.008)	0.0227 (0.0103)	0.0181 (0.011)	0 (0.0104)
Inaction rate	0.0896 (0.058)	0 (0.049)	0.0548 (0.048)	0 (0.066)

4.4 Conclusion

In view of the rapid developments in automobile electronics, what types of capital adjustment costs did they raise in auto-parts suppliers? We conjectured that GPT requires auto-parts suppliers to learn through capital-embodied technological progress. We explored quantitatively the effects of automobile electronics on capital adjustment costs, either convex/non-convex, or irreversible functions. Following Cooper and Haltiwanger (2006), we estimated via the simulated method of moments the Bellman equations for plants' dynamic optimization with respect to tangible capital, where there are decisions of inaction, buy, or sell capitals to choose discretely.

Though our estimates show a lack of stability in the coefficients, the effects of automobile electronics are mixed, if any. For the overall sample of auto-parts suppliers, there are no adjustment costs in any form, neither convex/non-convex, nor irreversible. As for the sectoral plants where automobile electronics seems embodied in the tangible capitals, we clearly detect a significant existence of the convex adjustment costs. Regarding another type of adjustment costs, on the one hand, the sell price of used capitals is anomalously higher than the buy price, which means auto electronics makes investment decision reversible. On the other hand, the fixed costs of plant restructuring, worker retraining, or organizational restructuring emerge, especially in the form of costs proportional to the plant size rather than an opportunity cost of investment. The nature of adjustment costs associated with auto electronics implies economic policy measures that should be taken in order to compensate for the output losses from capital adjustment costs in the face of general purpose technologies.

References

Arellano, M., & Bond, S. (1991). Some tests of specification for panel data: Monte Carlo evidence and an application to employment equations. *Review of Economic Studies, 58*(2), 277–297.

Bloom, N., Schankerman, M., & Van Reenen, J. (2007). *Identifying technology spillovers and product market rivalry* (Vol. 13060). NBER Working Papers.

Blundell, R., & Bond, S. (1998). Initial conditions and moment restrictions in dynamic panel data models. *Journal of Econometrics, 87*(1), 115–143.

Bresnahan, T. F., & Trajtenberg, M. (1995). General purpose technologies "Engines of growth"? *Journal of Econometrics, 65*(1), 83–108.

Christiano, L., Eichenbaum, M., & Evans, C. (2005). Nominal rigidities and the dynamic effects of a shock to monetary policy. *Journal of Political Economy, 113*(1), 1–45.

Cooper, R., & Ejarque, J. (2003). Financial frictions and investment: Requiem in Q. *Review of Economic Dynamics, 6*(4), 710–728.

Cooper, R. W., & Haltiwanger, J. C. (2006). On the nature of capital adjustment costs. *Review of Economic Studies, 73*(3), 611–633.

David, P. (1990). The dynamo and the computer: An historical perspective on the modern productivity paradox. *American Economic Review, 80*(2), 355–361.

Eberly, J., Rebelo, S., & Vincent, N. (2006). *Investment and value: A neoclassical benchmark.* NBER Working Paper #13866.

Fackler, P., & Tastan, H. (2008). *A framework for indirect inference.* https://www.researchgate.net/profile/Paul-Fackler/publication/265449612_A_Framework_for_Indirect_Inference/links/54cba6990cf24601c08849ae/A-Framework-for-Indirect-Inference.pdf

Greenwood, J., Hercowitz, Z., & Krusell, P. (1997). Long-run implications of investment-specific technological change. *American Economic Review, 87*(3), 342–362.

Griffith, R., Harrison, R., & Van Reenen, J. (2006). How special is the special relationship? Using the impact of US R&D spillovers on UK firms as a test of technology sourcing. *American Economic Review, 96*(5), 1859–1875.

Griliches, Z. (1990). Patent statistics as economic indicators: A survey. *Journal of Economic Literature, 28*(4), 1661–1707.

Hayashi, F. (1982). Tobin's marginal q and average q: A neoclassical interpretation. *Econometrica, 50*(1), 213–224.

Hidalgo, C. (2015). *Why information grows: The evolution of order, from atoms to economies.* Basic Books.

Hornstein, A., & Krusell, P. (1996). Can technology improvements cause productivity slowdowns? In B. Bernanke & J. J. Rotemberg (Eds.), *NBER macroeconomics annual 1996* (pp. 209–259). MIT Press.

JIP Database (2010). *JIP Database*, https://www.rieti.go.jp/en/database/JIP2010/index.html.

Jovanovic, B., & Rousseau, P. (2005). General purpose technologies. In P. Aghion & S. Durlauf (Eds.), *Handbook of economic growth* (Vol. 1b, pp. 1181–1224. Elsevier BV

Justiniano, A., & Primiceri, G. E. (2008). The time-varying volatility of macroeconomic fluctuations. *American Economic Review, 98*(3), 604–641.

Penrose, E. (1959). *The theory of the growth of the firm.* John Wiley.

Roodman, D. (2006). How to do Xtabond2: An introduction to difference and system GMM in Stata. *The Stata Journal, 9*, 86–136.
Tauchen, G. (1986). Finite state Markov-chain approximations to univariate and vector autoregressions. *Economics Letters, 20*(2), 177–181.
Tauchen, G., & Hussey, R. (1991). Quadrature-based methods for obtaining approximate solutions to nonlinear asset pricing models. *Econometrica, 59*(2), 371–396.
Tokuda, A., & Saeki, Y. (2007a). The automobile electronics (1): A market analysis of in-vehicle electronically-controlled system (in Japanese). *Ritsumeikan Business Journal, 46*(2), 85–102.
Tokuda, A., & Saeki, Y. (2007b). The automobile electronics (2): A market analysis of in-vehicle electronically-controlled system (in Japanese). *Ritsumeikan Business Journal, 46*(3), 55–90.
Tokuda, A., & Saeki, Y. (2007c). The automobile electronics (3): A market analysis of in-vehicle electronically-controlled system (in Japanese). *Ritsumeikan Business Journal, 46*(3), 239–276.
Tonogi, K., Nakamura, J., & Asako, K. (2010). Estimation of multiple q models of investment: Investment behavior over heterogeneous capital goods during the period of excess capacity reduction (in Japanese). *Economics Today*. Research Institute of Capital Formation, Development Bank of Japan, 31(2).
Uzawa, H. (1969). Time preference and the Penrose effect in a two-class model of economic growth. *Journal of Political Economy*, 77(4, Part 2), 628–652.
Windmeijer, F. (2005). A finite sample correction for the variance of linear efficient two-step GMM estimators. *Journal of Econometrics, 126*(1), 25–51.
YANO Research. (2009). *In-vehicle semiconductor market 2009 & 2010 (in Japanese).*

Chapter 5
Legal Enforcements for Competition Policy

Contents

Abstract Do legal enforcements for competition policy have differential effects on innovative research and development (R&D) activities? Considering both strategic R&D competition between incumbents and entrants, and the government's optimal choice of legal schemes, we first present a game-theoretic model of innovation and legal enforcement (Glaeser and Shleifer, Journal of Economic Literature 41:401–425, 2003; Schwartzstein and Shleifer, Journal of Law and Economics 56:1–38, 2013; Segal and Whinston, American Economic Review 97:1703–1730, 2007). The model suggests that there are in subgame-perfect equilibria some relations concerning average treatment effects of legal enforcement on the entrant's R&D or incumbent's deterrence activities, conditional on the law and order degree in the host country (World Bank Worldwide Governance Indicators*)*. Second, focusing on overseas

This chapter is based on Takeda and Uchida "Innovation and Legal Enforcement for Competition Policy: Theory and international evidence from overseas subsidiaries of the Japanese auto-parts suppliers," RIETI Discussion Paper Series 15-E-046, conducted as a part of the Project "East Asian Industry Productivity" undertaken at the Research Institute of Economy, Trade and Industry (RIETI). We use micro data pertaining to the *Basic Survey of Overseas Business Activities* and the *Basic Survey of Japanese Business Structure and Activities*, both conducted by the Ministry of Economy, Trade and Industry. The authors are grateful for helpful comments and suggestions by Masahisa Fujita, Kyoji Fukao, Shin-ichi Fukuda, Masaharu Hanazaki, Hidehiko Ishihara, Masayuki Morikawa, Junichi Nakamura, Mariko Tanaka, and the discussion paper seminar participants at RIETI.

Y. Takeda and I. Uchida, *Information Agglomeration of Japanese Auto Parts Suppliers*,
https://doi.org/10.1007/978-981-19-3300-4_5

subsidiaries of Japanese auto-parts suppliers that have international deployments with different legal origins in locations, we use a pooled data set of the *Basic Survey of Overseas Business Activities* and the *Basic Survey of Japanese Business Structure and Activities*. The average multi-valued treatment effect estimation shows positive results for the model. It suggests that under regulation as a legal enforcement scheme instead of strict liability or negligence, even in countries with a low degree of law and order, R&D activities would be more enhanced and R&D-deterrent ones be further suppressed on an average. Legal enforcement for competition policy does matter for innovation.

Keywords Innovation · R&D · Legal enforcement · Law and order

5.1 Introduction

Making strides across the great divide on competition and innovation between Schumpeter (1942) and Arrow (1962), as explained in Sect. 1.2.4 of Chap. 1, the Organisation for Economic Co-operation and Development (OECD) has recently launched indicators of product market regulation, especially a set of indicators on competition law and policies to characterize competition regimes (Alemani et al., 2016). The indicators can be seen as a recognition for Arrow (1962), that is, a competitive product market allows new entrants to challenge incumbents, efficient firms to grow, and inefficient ones to exit, thereby boosting economic growth.

However, regarding how competition policy, including an antitrust law, fosters innovation, the great divide still remains unsolved in industrial organizations or economic growth fields (Baker, 2007; Shapiro, 2012). Especially, as Baker (2007) suggested from a viewpoint of law and economics, "antitrust is not a general purpose competition intensifier. Rather, antitrust intervention can be focused on industry setting and categories of behavior where enforcement can promote innovation." (p. 589). Hence, we have to evaluate the role of antitrust as a competition policy (Buccirossi et al., 2013), based on a dynamic model of competition for the market (Evans & Schmalensee, 2002) that takes into account both ex-ante and ex-post market structure.

Following the literature reviewed in Sect. 1.2.4 of Chap. 1, this chapter considers a role of legal enforcement for competition policy in lowering transaction costs associated with organizational links for information agglomeration, as introduced in Chap. 1 and Hidalgo (2015). Our theoretical question is: do legal enforcements for competition policy have differential effects on innovative R&D activities? To find an answer, we should consider the government's optimal choice of legal schemes, as well as strategic R&D competition between incumbents and entrants.

This chapter also empirically evaluates the theoretical question above, especially testable hypotheses derived from a game-theoretic model constructed, on relations between R&D or R&D-deterring activities, and the degree of law and order in the host country. Our data include overseas subsidiaries of Japanese auto-parts suppliers.

Table 5.1 Host countries: *Basic Survey of Overseas Business Activities*

Ranking	2003	2004	2005
1	US (262)	US (266)	US (301)
2	Thailand (149)	China (163)	China (225)
3	China (130)	Thailand (142)	Thailand (166)
4	Indonesia (71)	Indonesia (77)	Indonesia (79)
5	Taiwan (48)	Taiwan (47)	India (48)
6	India (44)	Malaysia (45)	Taiwan (47)
7	Republic of Korea (41)	India (41)	Republic of Korea (44)
8	Malaysia (39)	Republic of Korea (41)	Philippines (39)
9	Philippines (39)	UK (37)	Malaysia (36)
10	UK (37)	Philippines (35)	UK (36)
Total	1156	1197	1321

The auto-parts industry includes innovative products represented by "hybrid" engines, where "as modularity becomes an established way of doing business, competition among module suppliers will intensify. Assemblers will look for the best-performing or lowest cost modules, spurring these increasingly sophisticated and independent suppliers into a race for innovation similar to the one already happening with computer modules." (Baldwin & Clark, 1997; Frigant, 2009). Japanese auto-parts suppliers have entered countries that maintain a high degree of law and order and have "legal origin historically transplanted," and frequently face antitrust lawsuits with enormous reparations.[1] From our data of the *Basic Survey of Overseas Business Activities* containing country-specific variations in legal enforcement schemes, the time-varying international dispersion of host countries is indicated in Table 5.1 with the number of samples in parenthesis. Among the top 10 host countries from 2003 to 2005, the US, UK, Thailand, India, and Malaysia have common law traditions, while China, Taiwan, and the Republic of Korea are under the German legal origin of civil law, and Indonesia and the Philippines under the French civil law.

This chapter is structured as follows: Sect. 5.2 explains a simple model of innovation and legal enforcement for competition policy, mentioning setup, subgame-perfect equilibria, and testable hypotheses. Section 5.3 describes our data and estimation method, and reports the estimation results. Finally, we conclude with Sect. 5.4.

[1] We will not deal with actual antitrust lawsuits concerning Japanese auto-parts suppliers, especially in the US. However, one of the intriguing topics would be the effects on innovation of a change in corporate leniency policy, which was introduced in the US in 1978 (the first amnesty program) and in 1993 (revised for giving more incentives to report spontaneously); in the EU in 1996 and in 2002 (similarly modified); in Japan in 2006; and in Mexico, Canada, South Korea, and Australia among over 40 countries. Recently, such lawsuits have also become rampant in China and India.

5.2 A Simple Model of Innovation and Legal Enforcement for Competition Policy

We present a simple model of legal enforcement in a winner-takes-all R&D competition for product innovation, where we consider both strategic R&D competition between an incumbent and a potential entrant, and the government's optimal choice of legal schemes for competition policy.

First, we construct a setup of the R&D competition consisting of two equal-sized firms, an incumbent, and another potential entrant. They play an R&D competition game, whose winner would enjoy monopoly profits. While a potential entrant does R&D activities for raising a probability of successful innovation, an incumbent deters the entrant's R&D activities, preventing the entrant from getting patent license for a purpose of compatibility or standardization, or committing to practices or illegal means difficult for courts or regulators to detect. A benevolent government, including a judge and regulator, also maximizes expected social profits from innovation, with a choice of a legal scheme among either strict liability, negligence, or regulation in a one-period game.

The game starts with the government's choice of a legal scheme at a timing 0, followed by the incumbent's R&D-deterring activities at a timing 1, the entrant's R&D activities at a timing 2, and innovation outcome and occurrence of either legal enforcement or subversion at a timing 3. A possibility of subversion at the final stage is incorporated into the model since an incumbent has to invest a maximum fine enforceable without subversion. If the maximum fine is lower than the actual fine paid by an incumbent, the incumbent subverts justice instead of submitting to the law.

Next, we show subgame-perfect equilibria of the game, each with or without possible subversion. Without the government's choice of a legal scheme, there are no Nash (pure-strategy) equilibria concerning strategies of an incumbent and an entrant, assuming that R&D activities of a potential entrant would be socially efficient without an incumbent's R&D-deterrence. The assumption is a rationale of antitrust policy for potential entrants.

Finally, we induce some testable hypotheses on relationships among observable variables. The model suggests a step-like positive relation between R&D activities and the degree of law and order in the host country, controlling the firm's scale, and so on. It also implies a step-like negative relation between R&D deterrence activities and the degree of law and order. These relations are tested in the next section using a panel dataset of overseas subsidiaries of Japanese auto-parts suppliers.

5.2.1 *Setup of a Winner-Takes-All R&D Competition*

There are two equal-sized firms, one is an incumbent and the other is a potential entrant with the same firm-scale S. If the entrant gets a patent through successful innovation, the incumbent gets displaced. But, if innovation fails, the monopoly of the incumbent continues.

In an R&D competition between the incumbent and entrant, on the one hand, a potential entrant conducts R&D activities R_1or$R_2(> R_1)$ for raising the probability of a successful innovation. The investment R_1 costs zero, with a probability of success P_1, while the R_2 does SC with a result of a higher probability $P_2(> P_1)$.

On the other hand, an incumbent conducts "R&D-deterring" activities Q_1or$Q_2(> Q_1)$ with the purpose of preventing patent license, compatibility, standardization, and so on. The deterrence activities Q_1 take zero cost with no effect on the success probability of the entrant's R&D activities. However, the higher deterrence Q_2 costs SC, lowering the entrant's probability of innovation down to P_1.

The winner of the competition takes all the monopoly profits of the incumbent, defined as $SE = SD-$ R&D-deterring or R&D activity costs, where SD denotes social profits of innovation. Each firm maximizes expected profits minus the R&D or R&D-deterring cost, minus the expected fine for the incumbent or entrant.

Note that we assume the parameters to satisfy a condition:

Condition 1 $(\mathbf{P}_2 - \mathbf{P}_1)\mathbf{D} > \mathbf{C}$

It is assumed to be socially efficient for an entrant to take R_2 without the incumbent's R&D-deterrence, which should be the rationale for an antitrust policy for the entrant.

The government also plays a role of choosing a legal enforcement scheme for antitrust. By government, we mean a judge or a regulator. The government can detect a high R&D-deterring incumbent with an exogenous probabilityP_D, and a low R&D entrant with another exogenous probabilityP_L. We assume another condition.

Condition 2 $\mathbf{P}_D < \mathbf{P}_L$

Based on an intuitive interpretation of more difficulty in detecting R&D deterrence than low R&D activities themselves. The probability of detecting the incumbent's R&D-deterring activities is also assumed to be low enough so that.

Condition 3 $(1 - \mathbf{P}_1)\mathbf{P}_D < \mathbf{P}_2 - \mathbf{P}_1,$

Which determines a minimum level of law and order required for attaining the first-best outcome under a legal enforcement scheme of negligence, as will be shown later.

There are three pure law enforcement schemes, each requiring fine F, in case. We define each scheme for legal enforcement as follows:

Definition 4 *Legal Enforcement Schemes.*

1. *Strict Liability*: *Government requires fines for both incumbent and entrant, any time innovation fails.*
2. *Negligence*: *Government fines either incumbent or entrant, if there are no innovations in high R&D-deterring activities or low R&D activities, respectively.*

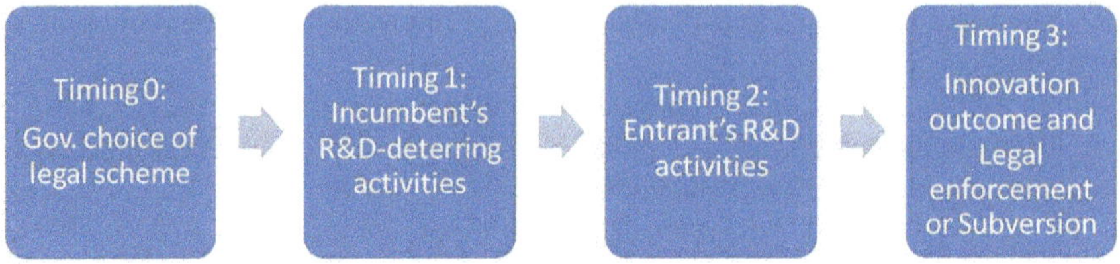

Fig. 5.1 Sequence of one-period game

3. *Regulation*: *Government fines either incumbent or entrant, if there are high R&D-deterring activities or low R&D activities, respectively.*

One is "strict liability," where the government requires fines for both incumbent and entrant, any time no innovations occur. Second, "negligence" fines either incumbent or entrant, if no innovations in high R&D-deterring activities or low R&D activities, respectively. Third, "regulation" fines either incumbent or entrant, if high R&D-deterring activities or low R&D activities are found, respectively.[2] We also call as "anarchy" a state with neither scheme. Each of the three schemes is chosen by a benevolent government maximizing expected social profits from successful innovation, minus R&D and R&D-deterring costs. In this setup, the first-best outcome is generated where an incumbent chooses Q_1 and an entrant doesR_2, while the second-best is a combination of Q_2 andR_2.

We next introduce into the model a possibility of subversion, which by paying a maximum fine X is enforceable without subversion for lobbying or corruption, for instance; then the incumbent could obviate for protection from law. If X is lower than the fine actually paid, the incumbent could subvert justice than submit to the law. Higher X possesses higher levels of "law and order."

Finally, a sequence of the R&D competition game is shown in Fig. 5.1. At a timing 0, the government chooses a legal scheme that maximizes the expected social profits from subsequent activities of the incumbent's R&D-deterrence and entrant's R&D investment. Until the final stage of timing 3, there remains a possibility of subversion for the incumbent.

[2] In considering effects of corporate leniency policy, we may make changes in legal enforcement in such a way that negligence fines both the incumbent and entrant if there are no innovations either in high R&D-deterring activities or low R&D activities, while regulation fines both the incumbent and entrant if either high R&D-deterring activities or low R&D activities are found. It is to be seen in the near future how there might be some changes in the relationship between R&D or R&D-deterring activities and law and order when introducing corporate leniency policy in the countries concerned.

5.2.2 *Subgame-Perfect Equilibria of Incumbent and Entrant Activities*

We show subgame-perfect equilibria of the game in each case without or with possible subversion, in due order below. Though our primary interest is in a case with possible subversion, the world free from possible subversion would be a reference case to our reality replete with lobbying or corruption.

5.2.2.1 Case Without Possible Subversion

We start with a state of anarchy where neither litigation nor regulation exists. In anarchy, the entrant's best responses at a timing 2 are R_2 to the incumbent's Q_1, and R_1 to the incumbent's Q_2. Then the incumbent's expected profits at a timing 1 are $(1 - P_2)SD$ if a lower deterrence level Q_1 is chosen, or $(1 - P_1)SD - SC$ if Q_2 is chosen. It is obtained that $(1 - P_1)SD - SC > (1 - P_2)SD$ from Condition 1, so that the worst outcome of a choice (Q_2, R_1) is always attained.

Next, we consider best responses under one litigation case of strict liability. Then the entrant's best responses at timing 2 are R_2 to the incumbent's actionQ_1, and R_1 toQ_2. The best responses generate the incumbent's expected profit at timing 1, $(1 - P_2)(SD - F)$ in case of choice Q_1 or $(1 - P_1)(SD - F) - SC$ in choiceQ_2. The first-best outcome from a pair of choice (Q_1, R_2) is attained ifz

$$\frac{F}{S} > \frac{(P_2 - P_1)D - C}{P_2 - P_1}.$$

In the other litigation case of negligence, the entrant's best responses at timing 2 are R_2 to the incumbent's actionQ_1, but when an incumbent takesQ_2, R_1 if

$$\frac{F}{S} < \frac{C}{(1 - P_1)P_L}$$

or R_2 otherwise. Then the incumbent's expected profits at timing 1 are $(1 - P_2)SD$ if an action Q_1 is taken or $(1 - P_1)(SD - P_D F) - SC$ if Q_2 is done. As a result, the first-best pair of choice (Q_1, R_2) is attained if

$$\frac{F}{S} > \frac{(P_2 - P_1)D - C}{(1 - P_1)P_D}.$$

Similarly, we pick up a case of regulation, where the entrant's best responses are R_2 to the incumbent's choiceQ_1, and to the incumbent'sQ_2, R_1 if

$$\frac{F}{S} < \frac{C}{P_L}$$

or R_2 otherwise. Then the incumbent's expected profits are $(1 - P_2)SD$ for Q_1 or $(1 - P_1)SD - P_D F - SC$ for Q_2. The first-best (Q_1, R_2) is attained if

$$\frac{F}{S} > \frac{(P_2 - P_1)D - C}{P_D}.$$

Considering the best responses under each legal scheme, a benevolent government decides which schemes are optimal in terms of maximization of the expected social profits.

We summarize the subgame-perfect equilibria in a case without possibility of subversion. We classify the parameters into the following three cases: case 1: $\frac{C}{P_L} > \frac{(P_2-P_1)D-C}{P_D}$; case 2: $\frac{C}{P_L} < \frac{(P_2-P_1)D-C}{P_D} < \frac{C}{(1-P_1)P_L}$; case 3: $\frac{C}{(1-P_1)P_L} < \frac{(P_2-P_1)D-C}{P_D}$. In each case, depending on some thresholds of the fine relative to the firm scale $\frac{F}{S}$, there exists a different subgame-perfect equilibria.

Proposition 5 *Without any possibility of subversion, there are such subgame-perfect equilibria in each case:*

1 *Case 1:* $\frac{C}{P_L} > \frac{(P_2-P_1)D-C}{P_D}$

(a) *For* $\frac{F}{S} < \frac{(P_2-P_1)D-C}{P_D}$, *the worst choice* (Q_2, R_1) *under anarchy.*
(b) *For* $\frac{(P_2-P_1)D-C}{P_D} < \frac{F}{S} < \frac{(P_2-P_1)D-C}{P_2-P_1}$, *the first-best* (Q_1, R_2) *under regulation.*
(c) *For* $\frac{(P_2-P_1)D-C}{P_2-P_1} < \frac{F}{S} < \frac{(P_2-P_1)D-C}{(1-P_1)P_D}$, *the first-best* (Q_1, R_2) *under regulation or strict liability.*
(d) *For* $\frac{(P_2-P_1)D-C}{(1-P_1)P_D} < \frac{F}{S}$, *the first-best* (Q_1, R_2) *under either of legal enforcement schemes.*

2 *Case 2:* $\frac{C}{P_L} < \frac{(P_2-P_1)D-C}{P_D} < \frac{C}{(1-P_1)P_L}$

(a) *For* $\frac{F}{S} < \frac{C}{P_L}$, *the worst choice* (Q_2, R_1) *under anarchy.*
(b) *For* $\frac{C}{P_L} < \frac{F}{S} < \frac{(P_2-P_1)D-C}{P_D}$, *the second-best* (Q_2, R_2) *under regulation.*
(c) *For* $\frac{(P_2-P_1)D-C}{P_D} < \frac{F}{S} < \frac{(P_2-P_1)D-C}{P_2-P_1}$, *the first-best* (Q_1, R_2) *under regulation.*
(d) *For* $\frac{(P_2-P_1)D-C}{P_2-P_1} < \frac{F}{S} < \frac{(P_2-P_1)D-C}{(1-P_1)P_D}$, *the first-best* (Q_1, R_2) *under regulation or strict liability.*
(e) *For* $\frac{(P_2-P_1)D-C}{(1-P_1)P_D} < \frac{F}{S}$, *the first-best* (Q_1, R_2) *under either of legal enforcement schemes.*

3 *Case 3:* $\frac{C}{(1-P_1)P_L} < \frac{(P_2-P_1)D-C}{P_D}$

(a) *For* $\frac{F}{S} < \frac{C}{P_L}$, *the worst choice* (Q_2, R_1) *under anarchy.*
(b) *For* $\frac{C}{P_L} < \frac{F}{S} < \frac{C}{(1-P_1)P_L}$, *the second-best* (Q_2, R_2) *under regulation.*
(c) *For* $\frac{C}{(1-P_1)P_L} < \frac{F}{S} < \frac{(P_2-P_1)D-C}{P_D}$, *the second-best* (Q_2, R_2) *under regulation or negligence.*
(d) *For* $\frac{(P_2-P_1)D-C}{P_D} < \frac{F}{S} < \frac{(P_2-P_1)D-C}{P_2-P_1}$, *the first-best* (Q_1, R_2) *under regulation.*

(e) *For* $\frac{(P_2-P_1)D-C}{P_2-P_1} < \frac{F}{S} < \frac{(P_2-P_1)D-C}{(1-P_1)P_D}$, *the first-best* (Q_1, R_2) *under regulation or strict liability.*

(f) *For* $\frac{(P_2-P_1)D-C}{(1-P_1)P_D} < \frac{F}{S}$, *the first-best* (Q_1, R_2) *under either of legal enforcement schemes.*

Proof. See **Appendix**. Figures 5.2, 5.3, and 5.4 also indicate the results of **Proposition 5** graphically.

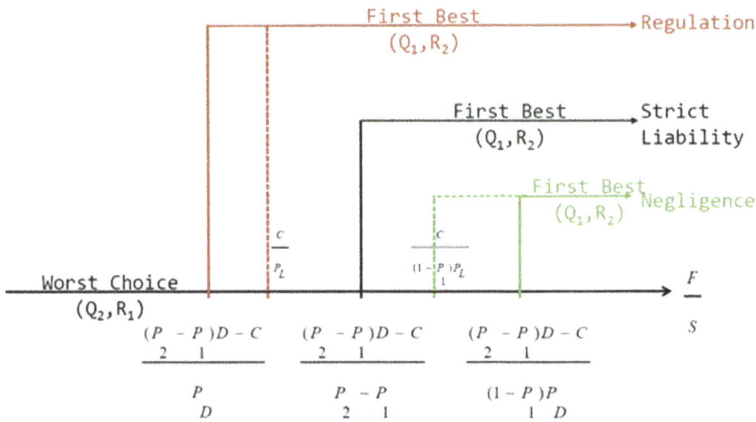

Fig. 5.2 Subgame-perfect equilibria without possible subversion: Case 1

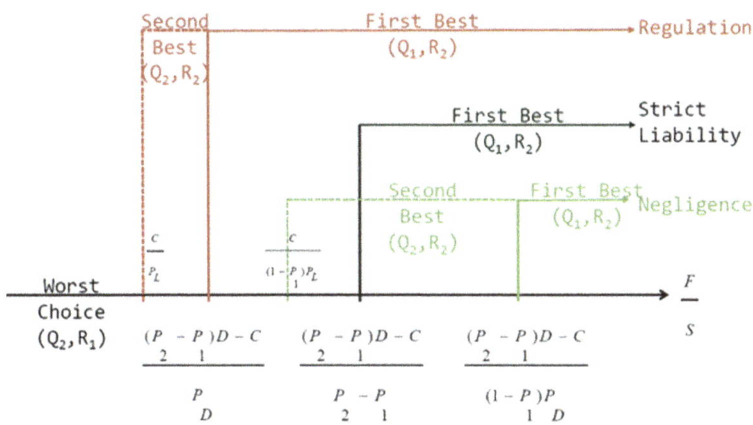

Fig. 5.3 Subgame-perfect equilibria without possible subversion: Case 2

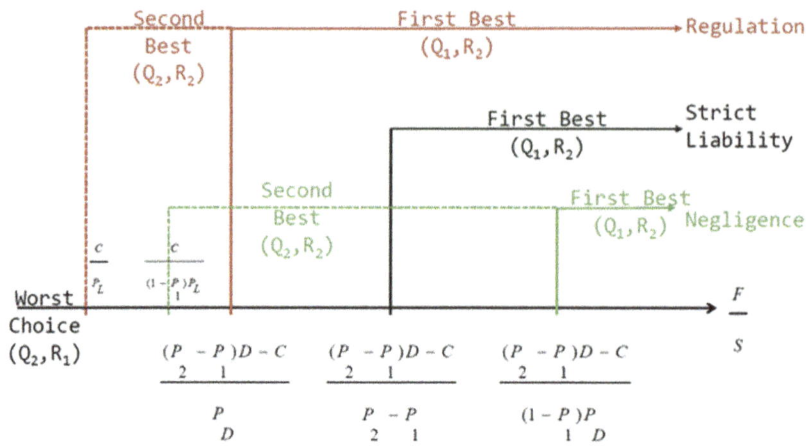

Fig. 5.4 Subgame-perfect equilibria without possible subversion: Case 3

5.2.2.2 Case with Possible Subversion

We consider a possibility of subversion at a timing 3 in a model. If the maximum fine enforceable without subversion X is smaller than actually paid fineF, then the incumbent would commit to subversion instead of observing law and order. Otherwise, either legal enforcement scheme chosen by the government can avoid subversion. Consequently, the possibility of subversion can give us another but similar proposition concerning a case with possible subversion, by simply replacing variable F with X in **Proposition 5**. Thus, with possible subversion, properties of subgame-perfect equilibria depend on the degree of law and order relative to firm scale$\frac{X}{S}$, in such a way indicated in Figs. 5.2, 5.3 and 5.4.

5.2.3 *Testable Hypotheses*

We induce from our game-theoretic model of R&D competition testable hypotheses on R&D and R&D-deterring activities of firms. Our hypotheses are testable on average effects of legal enforcement t on R&D or R&D-deterring activitiesy, conditional on a covariate, law and order variablex, once controlling firms' scale-variables. Consider each legal enforcement, either regulation, strict liability or negligence, as a treatment$k = 1, 2, 3$, respectively. Then with a random variation in law and order$\frac{X}{S}$, we measure average treatment effect on potential outcome y for the treated (thereafter, ATET)

$$E(y_i - y_j | t = k; x, s)$$

Table 5.2 Hypotheses on signs on ATET of R&D activities

$E(y_i - y_j \| t = k)$		Case		
K	(i,j)	1	2	3
1. Regulation	(1,2)	+	+	+
	(1,3)	+	+	+
	(2,3)	+	+	+
2. Strict liability	(1,3)	+	+	+
	(2,1)	0	0	0
	(2,3)	+	+	+
3. Negligence	(1,2)	0	0	+
	(3,1)	0	0	0
	(3,2)	0	0	+

for $i, j(\neq i), k = 1,2,3$.

For instance, let us take Case 1 depicted by Fig. 5.2. When a treatment of regulation is taken, the outcome of R&D activities $y_1 = R_2$ is always superior to another outcome y_2 ory_3; the potential outcome otherwise would be under strict liability or negligence, conditional on actual choice of regulation, that is, in a range of$\frac{(P_2-P_1)D-C}{P_D} < \frac{x}{s}$. If $\frac{(P_2-P_1)D-C}{P_D} < \frac{x}{s} < \frac{(P_2-P_1)D-C}{P_2-P_1}$, then potential outcome y_2 or y_3 would be R_1. If $\frac{(P_2-P_1)D-C}{P_2-P_1} < \frac{x}{s} < \frac{C}{(1-P_1)P_L}$, then it would be $y_2 = R_2$ but $y_3 = R_1$. If $\frac{C}{(1-P_1)P_L} < \frac{x}{s}$, then either outcome would be R_2. Average potential outcome of y_2 or y_3 conditional on a treatment of regulation i = 1 should be strictly smaller than one of y_1, so that ATET

$$E(y_1 - y_2 | t = 1; x, s) > 0$$

$$E(y_1 - y_3 | t = 1; x, s) > 0.$$

Similarly, we have $E(y_2 - y_3 | t = 1; x, s) > 0$. We summarize in Tables 5.2 and 5.3 hypothetical sign conditions on ATET of R&D and R&D-deterring activities.

5.3 Empirical Analysis

We proceed to empirical analysis to test two hypotheses implied from the theoretical model concerning R&D and R&D-deterrence activities. Sample firms should be active in innovative industries facing a-winner-takes-all competition. Our data include overseas subsidiaries of Japanese auto-parts suppliers. The sources of the panel data are the *Basic Survey of Overseas Business Activities* and *Basic Survey of Japanese Business Structure and Activities*, complied by the Ministry of Economy,

Table 5.3 Hypotheses on signs on ATET of R&D-deterring activities

$E(y_i - y_j \mid t = k)$		Case		
K	(i,j)	1	2	3
1. Regulation	(1,2)	–	–	–
	(1,3)	–	–	–
	(2,3)	–	–	–
2. Strict liability	(1,3)	–	–	–
	(2,1)	0	0	0
	(2,3)	–	–	–
3. Negligence	(1,2)	0	0	0
	(3,1)	0	0	0
	(3,2)	0	0	0

Trade and Industry, Japan. We cover the corporations belonging to two industrial classifications: motor vehicles, motor vehicle bodies, and trailers; and motor vehicle parts and accessories.

As for legal information in each host country where these corporations are located overseas, we take advantage of the indices concerning legal origins (La Porta et al., 2008) and legal procedures. Along with country data on the legal procedures, we also use some indices in the *World Bank Worldwide Governance Indicators* as data on the degree of law and order.

We estimate the step-like functions of either R&D expenses or overseas technical transfers relative to the law and order degree. The method is an estimator on average treatment effects via propensity score matching (Chapter 18 in Wooldridge, 2002). What we should note is our identification of legal enforcement schemes based on indices of both legal origins and efficiency of each judicial system.

5.3.1 Data

5.3.1.1 Pooled Data

Our pooled data on overseas subsidiaries of Japanese auto-parts suppliers consists of two sources: *Basic Survey of Overseas Business Activities* and *Basic Survey of Japanese Business Structure and Activities*. In the second source, "auto parts" mean two categories in industrial classification: motor vehicles, motor vehicle bodies, and trailers (no. 1601); and motor vehicle parts and accessories (no. 1602). Our annual sample is from 2003 to 2011.

In the first data source, we use R&D expenses for R_1 or R_2 and some proxies for a local subsidiary's scales: total sales; and local sales. After matching each individual corporation in both data sources, in the second source we can identify the amount of overseas technical transfer, which indicates the parent firm's receipts from patent licensees overseas. It closely stands for how *less deterrent* a subsidiary is to the R&D activities of rival competitors, a proxy variable for R&D-deterring activities Q_1 or Q_2 with a negative correlation. We also use in the second data source some controlling variables, such as total sales, current net profit, capital adequacy ratio, and foreign-owned capital ratio. Further to control how active a parent firm is in acquiring patent rights, we take advantage of a variable of patent rights maintained.

5.3.1.2 Law and Order Data

Regarding the degree of law and order X in each host country where these corporations are located overseas, we use some indices in the *World Bank Worldwide Governance Indicators* and *Transparency International Corruption Perceptions Index*. The following proxies for law and order are used alternatively in estimation:

(a) Control of corruption: "Capturing perceptions of the extent to which public power is exercised for private gain, including both petty and grand forms of corruption, as well as "capture" of the state by elites and private interests."
(b) Rule of law: "Capturing perceptions of the extent to which agents have confidence in and abide by the rules of society, and in particular the quality of contract enforcement, property rights, the police, and the courts, as well as the likelihood of crime and violence."
(c) Political stability and absence of violence/terrorism: "Capturing perceptions of the likelihood that the government will be destabilized or overthrown by unconstitutional or violent means, including politically motivated violence and terrorism."
(d) Regulatory Quality: "Capturing perceptions of the ability of the government to formulate and implement sound policies and regulations that permit and promote private sector development."
(e) Government Effectiveness: "Capturing perceptions of the quality of public services, quality of the civil service and degree of its independence from political pressures, quality of policy formulation and implementation, and credibility of the government's commitment to such policies."
(f) Voice and Accountability: "Capturing perceptions of the extent to which a country's citizens are able to participate in selecting their government, as well as freedom of expression, freedom of association, and a free media."

(g) Corruption Perceptions Index (Transparency International): "Based on how corrupt their public sector is perceived to be. A composite index—a combination of polls—drawing on corruption-related data collected by a variety of reputable institutions. Reflecting the views of observers from around the world, including experts living and working in the countries and territories evaluated."

5.3.2 *Estimation*

5.3.2.1 Identification of Legal Enforcement Schemes

A critical point in estimation is how to identify legal enforcement schemes in each host country. We use the legal-scheme identification in the legal origin theory advocated by La Porta et al. (2008) as a clue. Each country has a legal origin historically transplanted and evolving over time, either common law or civil law. In general, the overall role of the judiciary or courts in countries with common law traditions is likely to be stronger than in countries with civil law, because of the importance of precedent.[3] The general property of legal origins suggests that civil law countries may be identified as ones with a legal enforcement scheme of regulation. We follow a dummy variable of legal origins used by La Porta et al. (2008), indicating whether the legal origin of the company law or commercial code of the country is common law (i.e., English legal origin) or civil law (i.e., French, Socialist, German, and Scandinavian legal origins).

Concerning the identification of liability rules, strict liability, or negligence, in common law countries, we utilize data on the efficiency of judiciary procedures from the World Bank Doing Business report. Under the legal enforcement of negligence, which requires the government to detect liable activities, judiciary processes are likely to be less efficient. The index of enforcing contracts "assesses the efficiency of the judicial system by following the evolution of a commercial sale dispute over the quality of goods and tracking the time, cost and number of procedures involved from the moment the plaintiff files the lawsuit until payment is received."(World Bank, "What is Doing Business" *Development Economics*, 2015) We split our sample of country and year into two groups—negligence scheme or strict liability—applying a criterion above or below a median value of the index for all the countries with a common law origin.

[3] Another method for identification is to utilize a general saliency that property rights are required to be more secure under the English common law than under the French civil law (La Porta et al., Lopez-de-Silanes, Shleifer and Vishny, 1999). It can be interpreted as a higher PD of the government's detection rate of the incumbent's deterrence under civil law than under common law. As a result, Case 1 in text would be more probable under civil law, while Case 3 more probable under common law. Consequently, under common law, the second-best choice with the incumbent's high R&D-deterring activities is more likely.

5.3.2.2 Average Multi-Valued Treatment Effect Estimation

We estimate ATET via the average multi-valued treatment effect estimation consisting of a potential outcome model and treatment model. A linear potential outcome model has a dependent variable of either R&D expenses/total sales ratio, or amount of overseas technical transfer/total sales. Independent variables consist of each law and order variable x,TFP estimates from Levinson-Petrin productivity estimator, in addition to controlling firm-level variables, macroeconomic variables of each host country, real GDP growth rate, dependence ratio on foreign trade defined as a sum of import and export divided by GDP, and time dummies.

However, a treatment model is multinomial logit, whose independent variables are the same x variable as in the potential outcome model, macro variables, and time dummies. In both the estimated models, robust standard errors are used.

In Table 5.4 on R&D activities, shaded cells indicate the cases satisfying the hypothetical sign condition shown in Table 5.2, suggesting strong evidence of the theoretical model. Regarding estimation results on R&D-deterring activities in Table 5.5, we also infer that the model can explain the hypotheses on sign conditions on ATET in Table 5.3, though more weakly than in the case of R&D activities.

5.4 Conclusion

We presented a game-theoretic model of innovation and legal enforcement for competition policy. The model generates testable hypotheses on the signs of average effects of legal enforcement on the entrant's R&D or the incumbent's deterrence activities, conditional on the law and order degree in the host country. Average multi-valued treatment effect estimation, on the one hand, suggests strong evidence of the model in the case of R&D expenses, and on the other hand, a weaker evidence for explaining overseas technical transfer. The evidence implies that whatever scheme for competition policy achieves the first best is more likely in countries with higher law and order; this plays an implicit but substantial role in considerations of how antitrust laws foster innovation. Legal enforcement, therefore, does matter for innovation.

Table 5.4 Average multi-valued treatment effect estimation: Results on R&D expenses

$E(y_i - y_j \| t = k)$#5291		X: law & order (from World Bank, Worldwide Governance Indicators, if not specified)						
K	(i, j)	Control of corruption	Rule of law	Political stability and absence of violence/ terrorism	Regulatory quality	Corruption perceptions index (Transparency international)	Government effectiveness	Voice of accountability
1. Regulation	(1,2)	0.0008	0.0006	–0.0015	0.0009	0.0008	–0.0015	0.0038
	(1,3)	0.0016*	0.0022***	0.0009	0.0012	0.0016*	0.0018**	0.0031***
	(2,3)	0.0008	0.0017	0.0024	0.0003	0.0008	0.0032*	–0.0008
2.Strict Liability	(1,3)	0.0074**	0.0086**	0.0049**	0.0074*	0.0069**	0.0089**	0.0053**
	(2,1)	0.0079	0.0065	0.0105**	0.0074	0.0085	0.0062	0.0105**
	(2,3)	0.0153***	0.0151***	0.0153***	0.0147***	0.0154***	0.0151***	0.0157***
3.Negligence	(1,2)	–0.0025	–0.0027	–0.0049	–0.0024	–0.0030	–0.0027	–0.0054**
	(3,1)	–0.0033**	–0.0040**	–0.0020**	–00,024**	–0.0030**	–0.0037**	–0.0017
	(3,2)	–0.0058*	–0.0067*	–0.0069**	–0.0048*	–0.0060*	–0.0064**	–0.0071***

Table 5.5 Average multi-valued treatment effect estimation: Results on overseas technical transfer

$E(y_i - y_j \mid t = k)$#2006		X: law & order (from World Bank, Worldwide Governance Indicators, if not specified)						
K	(i, j)	Control of corruption	Rule of law	Political stability and absence of violence/ terrorism	Regulatory quality	Corruption perceptions index (Transparency International)	Government effectiveness	Voice of accountability
1.Regulation	(1,2)	0.0009**	0.0009***	0.0010***	0.0010***	0.0008**	0.0010***	0.0008*
	(1,3)	0.0003	0.0005*	–9.64e-06	0.0001	0.0003	0.0004	0.0007**
	(2,3)	–0.0005	–0.0004	–0.0010**	–0.0008**	–0.0005	–0.0006	–0.0001
2.Strict liability	(1,3)	–0.0002	–0.0005	0.0001	–0.0008	–0.0002	–0.0005	–0.0003
	(2,1)	0.0002	0.0003	0.0002	0.0002	0.0002	0.0002	0.0002
	(2,3)	1.22e-06	–0.0003	0.0002	–0.0005	0.0001	–0.0003	–0.0001
3.Negligence	(1,2)	0.0008**	0.0009**	0.0006	0.0009***	0.0008**	0.0009**	0.0012**
	(3,1)	–0.0002	–0.0003	–0.00001	–0.0001	–0.0002	–0.0003	–0.0005
	(3,2)	0.0006	0.0006	0.0006	0.0008**	0.0006	0.0006	0.0008

Appendix Proof of Proposition 5

Here we make a proof of **Proposition 5** on subgame-perfect equilibria of the R&D competition game under optimal legal enforcement schemes. We solve the game below, via backward induction.

A-1. First, we consider a case under anarchy decided by the government at a timing 0.

(a) When an incumbent takes Q_1 action at a timing 1, the best-response R&D activities chosen at a timing 2 would be R_2, since the expected profits which the R&D cost 0 or SC and the expected fine are excluded from the expected monopoly profits SD in case of a higher R&D investment R_2, $P_2\text{S}(\text{D} - \text{C}) - (1 - P_2)\text{SC} = \text{S}(P_2\text{D} - \text{C})$, is higher than those in case of a lower R_1, $P_1\text{S}(\text{D} - 0) + (1 - P_1)0 = P_1\text{SD}$, on account of **Condition 1**. Similarly, when an incumbent takes Q_2 action at a timing 1, the best response of the entrant would be R_1, since R_1′ s expected profits P_1SD are higher than R_2′ s $\text{S}(\text{P}_1\text{D} - \text{C})$.

(b) At a timing 1 in turn taking account of the entrant's best responses, an incumbent would choose the best response Q_2 since the expected profits less the R&D-deterrence cost, less the expected fine in case of Q_2, $P_1\text{S}(0 - \text{C}) + (1 - P_1)\text{S}(\text{D} - \text{C}) = \text{S}[(1 - P_1)\text{D} - \text{C})]$, are higher than those in case of Q_1, $P_2\text{S}(0 - 0) + (1 - P_2)\text{SD} = \text{S}(1 - P_2)\text{D}$, due to **Condition 1**.

A-2. Next, suppose that the government follows strict liability for legal enforcement at a timing 0.

(a) At a timing 2, an entrant's best responses are unqualifiedly decided. In response to an incumbent's choice Q_1, the entrant makes a decision R_2 comparing the expected profits in both choices $P_2\text{S}(\text{D} - \text{C}) + (1 - P_2)(0 - \text{SC} - \text{F}) = \text{S}(P_2\text{D} - \text{C}) - (1 - P_2)\text{F} > P_1S(D - 0) + (1 - P_1)(0 - F) = P_1SD - (1 - P_1)F$, while it makes a response R_1 to the incumbent choice Q_2, resulting in the expected profits $P_1SD - (1 - P_1)F$ in comparison with lower $\text{S}(\text{P}_1\text{D} - \text{C}) - (1 - \text{P}_1)\text{F}$ if taking R_2.
(b) Unlike the entrant's best responses, an incumbent's deterrence decision entails a qualification that in order to achieve the first-best outcome, it is sufficient for the incumbent to follow the activitiesQ_1. A comparison of the expected profits $(1 - P_2)(SD - F)$ from Q_1 or $(1 - P_1)(SD - F) - SC$ from Q_2 answers the best response of the incumbent, so that a qualifying condition for the first-best choices (Q_1, R_2) is

$$\frac{\boldsymbol{F}}{\boldsymbol{S}} > \frac{(\boldsymbol{P}_2 - \boldsymbol{P}_1)\boldsymbol{D} - \boldsymbol{C}}{\boldsymbol{P}_2 - \boldsymbol{P}_1} \tag{A.1}$$

A-3.Third, we presume that at a timing 0, the government settles on negligence, where it has to detect activities of the incumbent or entrant for anti-competition resulting in no innovations.

(a) The best responses of an entrant at a timing 2 is contingent on a qualification concerning a probability P_L of the government detecting the entrant's choice of lower R&D activities. In case of incumbent choice Q_1, a higher level of R&D activities R_2 is superior in the expected profits of the entrant to the lower one R_1, since the former gives the higher expected value $P_2S(D-C)+(1-P_2)[P_L(0-SC)-(1-P_L)SC] = S(P_2D-C)$ than the latter, $P_1(SD-0)+(1-P_1)[P_L(0-F)-(1-P_L)0] = P_1SD-(1-P_1)P_LF$, irrespective of anything but **Condition 1**. However, if an incumbent decides higher deterrence Q_2, the entrant's expected profits from either of the R&D activities R_1 or R_2 cannot be ranked without a qualification. In a comparison between the expected profits $P_1SD-(1-P_1)P_LF$ and $S(P_2D-C)$ from R_1 or R_2, respectively, the best response would be R_1 if

$$\frac{\boldsymbol{F}}{\boldsymbol{S}} < \frac{\boldsymbol{C}}{(1-\boldsymbol{P}_1)\boldsymbol{P}_L} \text{ or otherwise } \boldsymbol{R}_2 \tag{A.2}$$

(b) Under the negligence scheme, an incumbent also considers a detection probability P_D in deciding the best response to the entrant's actions. The expected profits are $(1-P_2)SD$ from the deterrence Q_1 or $S[(1-P_1)D-C]-(1-P_1)P_DF$ from Q_2. The best choices (Q_1, R_2) can be attained if

$$\frac{\boldsymbol{F}}{\boldsymbol{S}} > \frac{(\boldsymbol{P}_2-\boldsymbol{P}_1)\boldsymbol{D}-\boldsymbol{C}}{(1-\boldsymbol{P}_1)\boldsymbol{P}_D} \tag{A.3}$$

A-4. Finally, we consider a case of regulation set enforceable by the government at a timing 0. Similar to the negligence scheme, the best responses of an entrant and an incumbent depend on each detection probability for the government.

(a) An entrant's best response to an incumbent choice of Q_1 is R_2 in a straightforward way to compare the expected profits $S(P_2D-C)$ from R_2 and P_1SD-P_LF from R_1. However, the entrant's best response to Q_2 relies on the relative magnitude of the expected profits, P_1SD-P_LF for R_1 or $S(P_2D-C)$ for R_2. A higher R&D expenditure R_2 should be chosen, if

$$\frac{\boldsymbol{F}}{\boldsymbol{S}} > \frac{\boldsymbol{C}}{\boldsymbol{P}_L}. \tag{A.4}$$

(b) With an incumbent's decision-making, the relative magnitude of the expected profits $(1-P_2)SD$ for Q_1 and $S[(1-P_1)D-C]-P_DF$ for Q_2 matters. The incumbent takes Q_1 activities, if

$$\frac{\boldsymbol{F}}{\boldsymbol{S}} > \frac{(\boldsymbol{P}_2-\boldsymbol{P}_1)\boldsymbol{D}-\boldsymbol{C}}{\boldsymbol{P}_D}. \tag{A.5}$$

A-5. At a timing 0, a benevolent government decides which legal enforcement scheme to maximize for social profits, considering the best responses of both the entrant and the incumbent at the timing 2 and 1. The decision does depend on the relative magnitude of $\frac{F}{s}$ expressed by the inequalities (A.1), (A.2), (A.3), (A.4), and (A.5) above. Among the five threshold values, the magnitude relationships are trivial on $\frac{C}{P_L} < \frac{C}{(1-P_1)P_L}$ and $\frac{(P_2-P_1)D-C}{P_D} < \frac{(P_2-P_1)D-C}{(1-P_1)P_D}$. Therefore, we classify possible cases into case 1: $\frac{C}{P_L} > \frac{(P_2-P_1)D-C}{P_D}$; case 2: $\frac{C}{P_L} < \frac{(P_2-P_1)D-C}{P_D} < \frac{C}{(1-P_1)P_L}$; and case 3: $\frac{C}{(1-P_1)P_L} < \frac{(P_2-P_1)D-C}{P_D}$. In Figs. 5.2, 5.3, and 5.4, the subgame-perfect equilibria in each case would be evident.

References

Alemani, E., Klein, C., Koske, I., Vitale, C., & Wanner, I. (2016). New indicators of competition law and policy in 2013 for OECD and non-OECD Countries. OECD economics department Working Papers no. 1104. *International Law and Economics*, 59–102.

Arrow, K. (1962). Economic welfare and the allocation of resources to invention. In *the Universities-National Bureau Committee for Economic Research and the Committee on Economic Growth of the Social Science Research Councils (Ed.), The rate and direction of inventive activity: Economic and social factors* (pp. 609–626). Princeton University Press.

Baker, J. B. (2007). Beyond Schumpeter vs. Arrow: How antitrust fosters innovation. *Antitrust Law Journal, 74*, 575–602.

Balas, A., La Porta, R., Lopez-de-Silanes, F., & Shleifer, A. (2009). The divergence of legal procedures. *American Economic Journal: Economic Policy, 1*(2), 138–162.

Baldwin, C. Y., & Clark, K. B. (1997). Managing in an age of modularity. *Harvard Business Review, 75*(5), 84–93.

Buccirossi, P., Ciari, L., Duso, T., Spagnolo, G., & Vitale, C. (2013). Competition policy and productivity growth: An empirical assessment. *Review of Economics and Statistics, 95*(4), 1324–1336.

Cooter, R. D. (1991). Economic theories of legal liability. *Journal of Economic Perspectives, 5*(3), 11–30.

Djankov, S., La Porta, R., Lopez-de-Silanes, F., & Shleifer, A. (2003). Courts. *Quarterly Journal of Economics, 118*(2), 453–517.

Evans, D. S., & Schmalensee, R. (2002). Some economic aspects of antitrust analysis in dynamically competitive industries. In A. B. Jaffe, J. Lerner, & S. Stern (Eds.), *Innovation policy and the economy* (Vol. 2, pp. 1–49). MIT Press.

Frigant, V. (2009). Winners and losers in the auto parts industry: Trajectories followed by the main first tier suppliers over the past decade. In M. Freyssenet (Ed.), *The Second automobile revolution* (pp. 419–442). Palgrave MacMillan.

Gans, J. S. (2011). When is static analysis a sufficient proxy for dynamic considerations? Reconsidering antitrust and innovation. In J. Lerner & S. Stern (Eds.), *Innovation policy and the economy* (Vol. 11, pp. 55–78). MIT Press.

Glaeser, E. L., & Shleifer, A. (2003). The rise of the regulatory state. *Journal of Economic Literature, 41*(2), 401–425.

Hidalgo, C. (2015). *Why information grows: The evolution of order, from atoms to economies*. Basic Books.

Kolstad, C. D., Ulen, T. S., & Johnson, G. V. (1990). Ex post liability for harm vs. ex ante safety regulation: Substitute or complements? *American Economic Review*, 80(4), 888–901.

La Porta, R., Lopez-de-Silanes, F., Shleifer, A., & Vishny, R. W. (1999). The quality of government. *Journal of Law, Economics, and Organization, 15*(1), 222–279.

La Porta, R. L., Lopez-de-Silanes, F., & Shleifer, A. (2008). The economic consequences of legal origins. *Journal of Economic Literature, 46*(2), 285–332.

Schumpeter, J. (1942). *Capitalism, socialism and democracy*. Harper & Brothers.

Schwartzstein, J., & Shleifer, A. (2013). An activity-generating theory of regulation. *Journal of Law and Economics, 56*(1), 1–38.

Segal, I. R., & Whinston, M. D. (2007). Antitrust in innovative industries. *American Economic Review, 97*(5), 1703–1730.

Shapiro, C. (2012). Competition and innovation: Did Arrow hit the bull's eye? In J. Lerner & S. Stern (Eds.), *The rate & direction of economic activity revisited* (pp. 361–404). University of Chicago Press.

Shavell, S. (1980). Strict liability versus negligence. *Journal of Legal Studies, 9*(1), 1–25.

Shleifer, A. (2005). Understanding regulation. *European Financial Management, 11*(4), 439–451.

Shleifer, A. (2012). *The failure of judges and the rise of regulators*. MIT Press.

Wooldridge, J. M. (2002). *Econometric analysis of cross section and panel data*. MIT Press.

Index

Y. Takeda and I. Uchida, *Information Agglomeration of Japanese Auto Parts Suppliers*,
https://doi.org/10.1007/978-981-19-3300-4

www.ingramcontent.com/pod-product-compliance
Ingram Content Group UK Ltd.
Pitfield, Milton Keynes, MK11 3LW, UK
UKHW022209051026
15624UKWH00001B/84
9789811932991